FACIAL

Art Reflections

L F Peterson Ph.D.
Peterson Art Gallery
Volume 1
Copyright © 2019

As a cognitive psychologist, I am aware of the contributions of gestalt to the field of art creation and interpretation. Art and psychology encourage creative, novel synthesis. Perceptions are a flux of continually moving conscious and unconscious cognitions forming Multi Factorial Apperceptions. Artists capture subjective experience and observers form new experiences. The greater the ambiguity, the greater the opportunity for aesthetic growth and cognitive change. My art is both an expression of creativity and a mechanism for ambiguity to value-maximize opportunities for interaction and novel interpretation.

Where scientists seek to narrow interpretation, artists seek to employ the Look, See, and Think approach maximize interpretations of their work. Gestalt psychology illustrates how minds interpret similarity, proximity, symmetry, and figure ground to form order out of chaos. Color, shape, distance and density stimulate memories and complex ideas. Ambiguity demands new perspectives until Eureka, or cognitive consistency is achieved.

The following paintings in volume 1 were created over a two year period in 2017 through 2018. I employ a small brush under magnification to create my art renderings. I trust my paintings will stimulate new emotional and intellectual awareness and understanding. I will be publishing over 1200 paintings in the near future and trust you will follow my creative efforts through the various volumes.

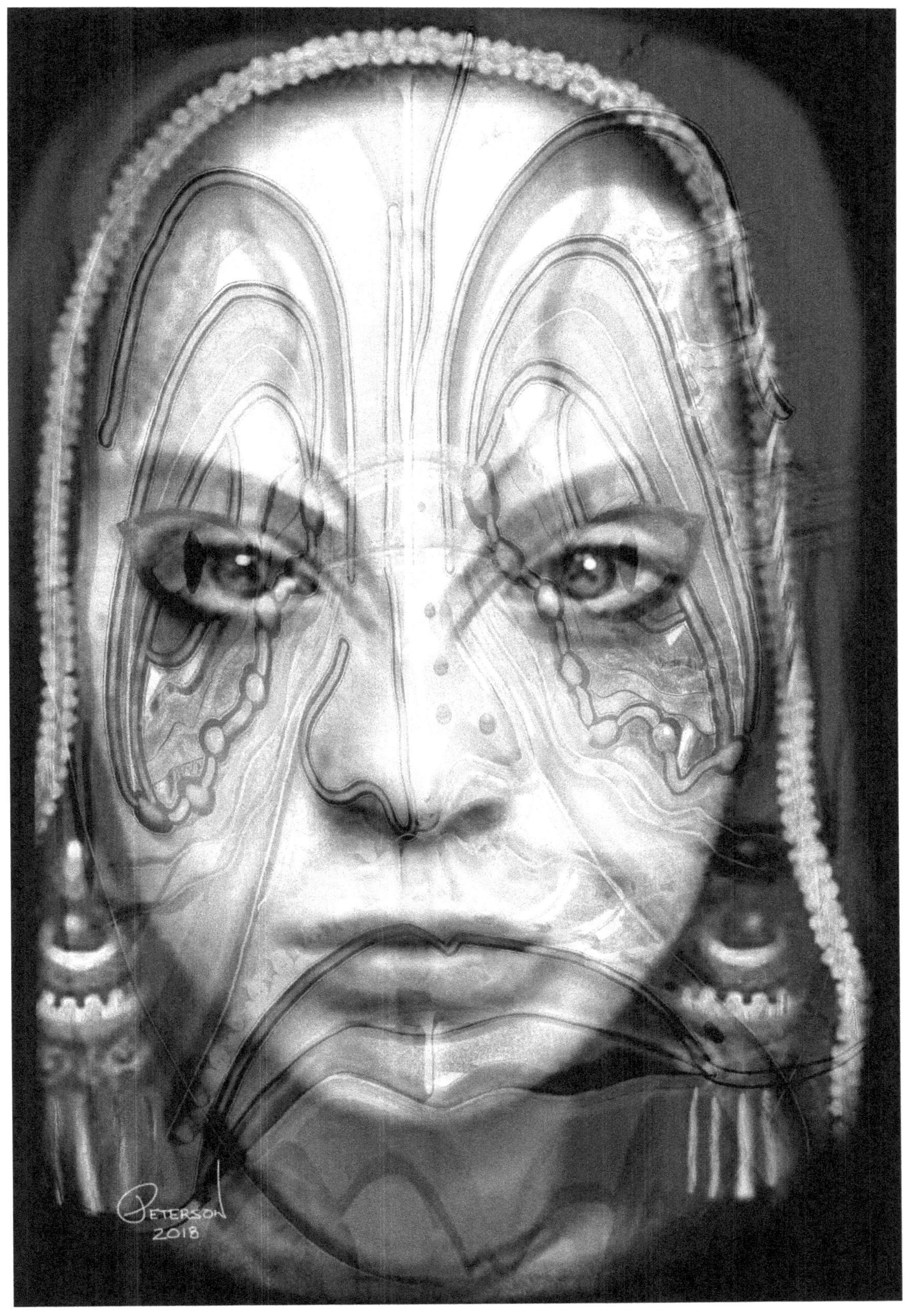

1

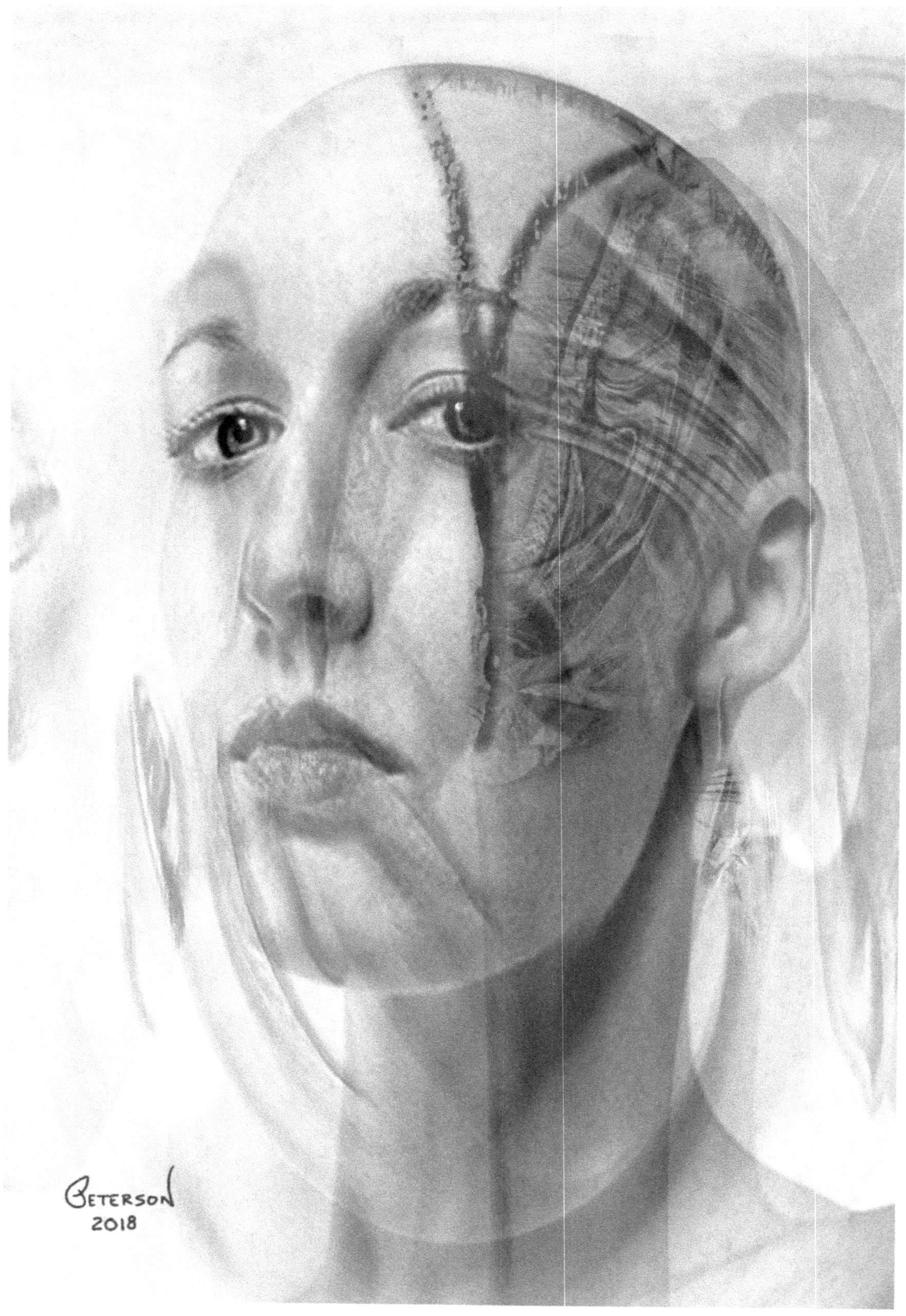

Peterson
2018

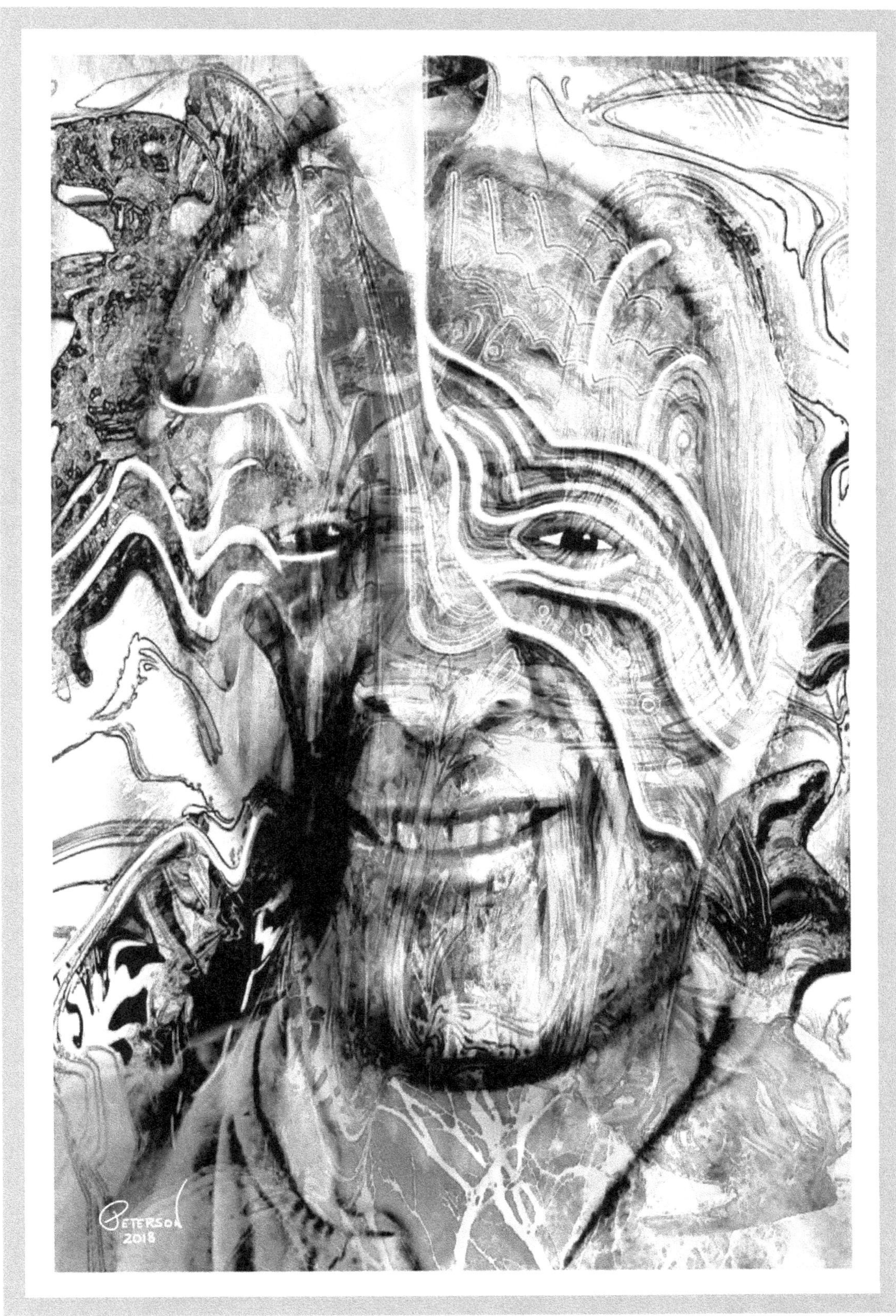
Peterson
2018

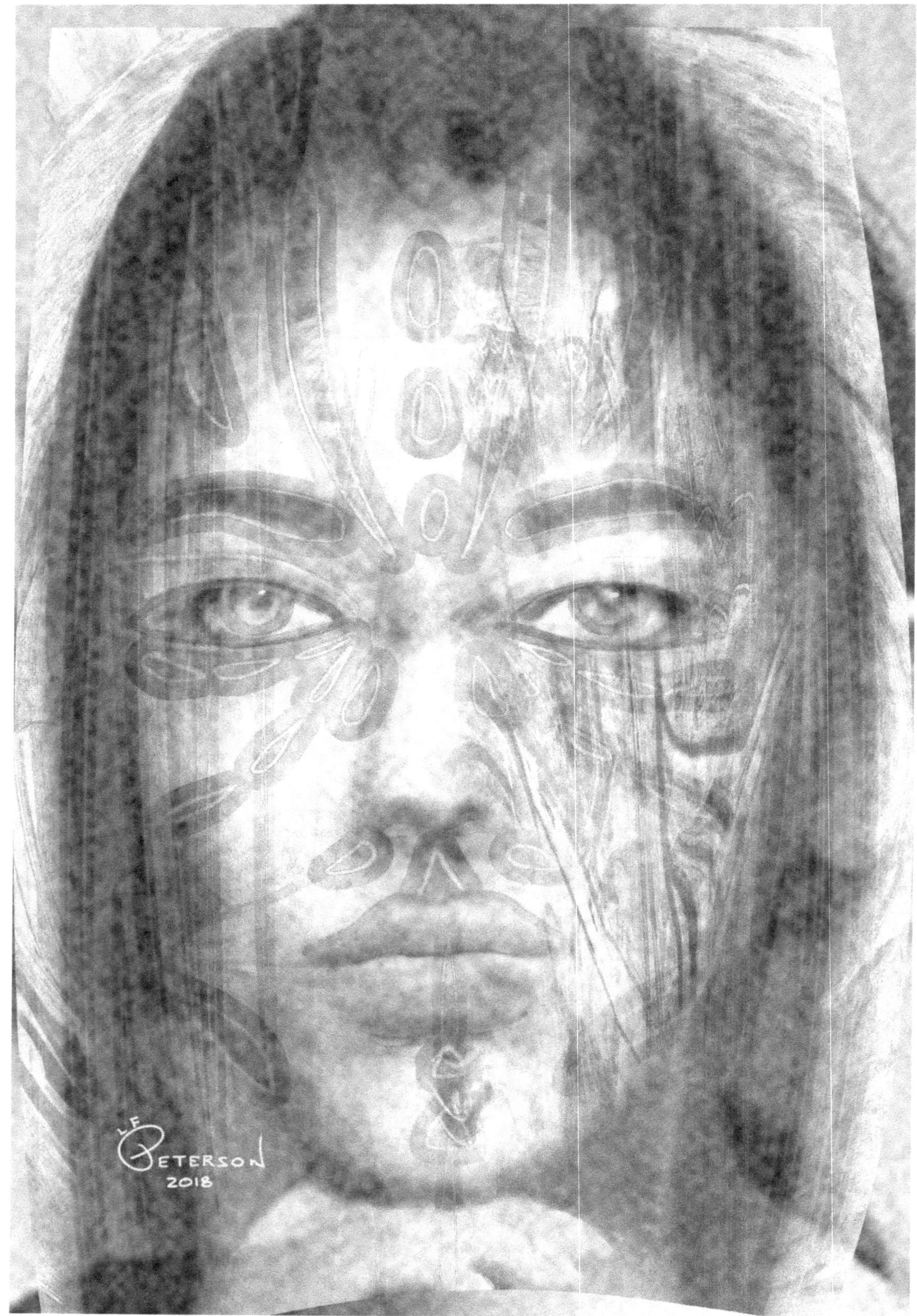
LF
PETERSON
2018

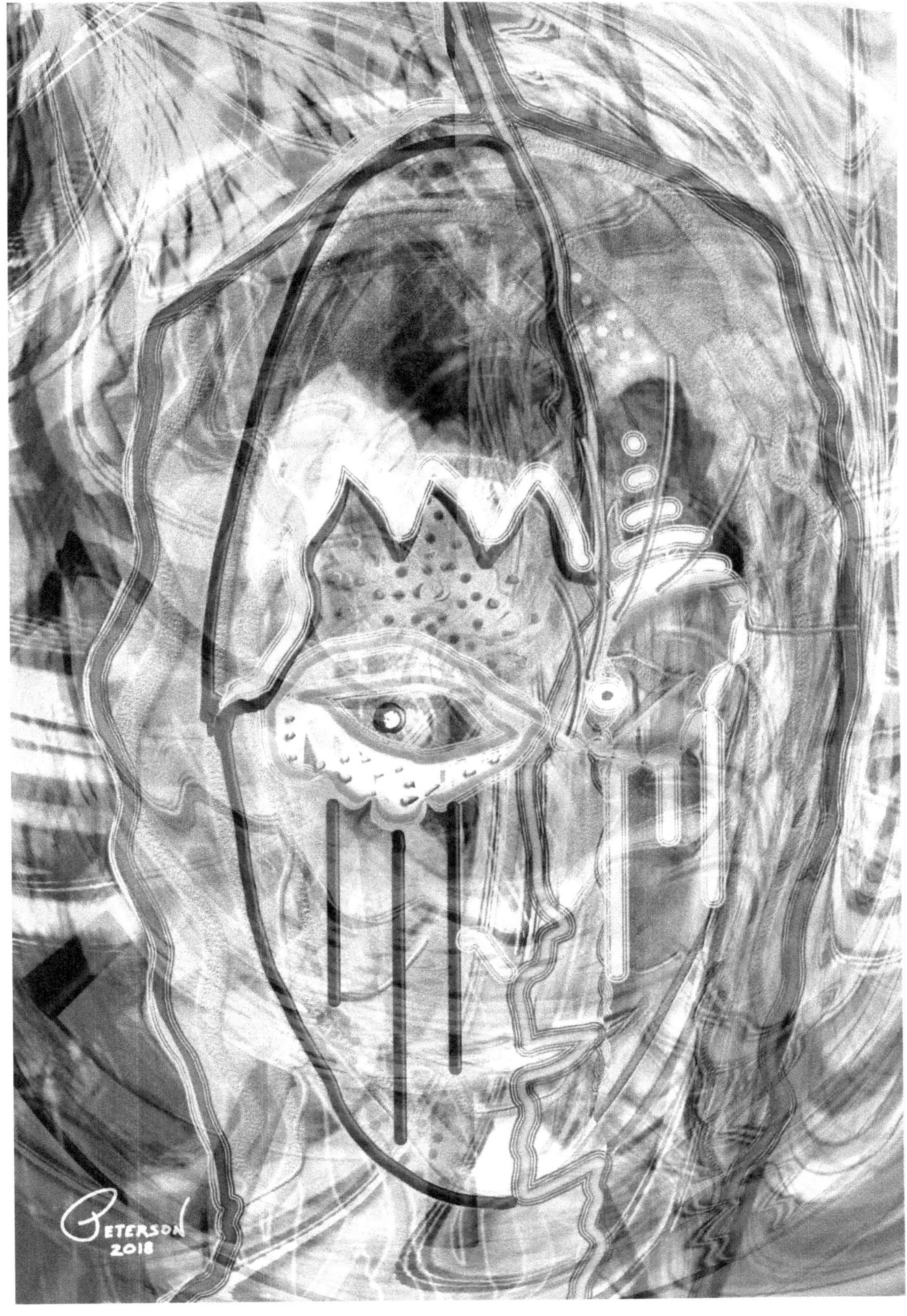
Peterson
2018

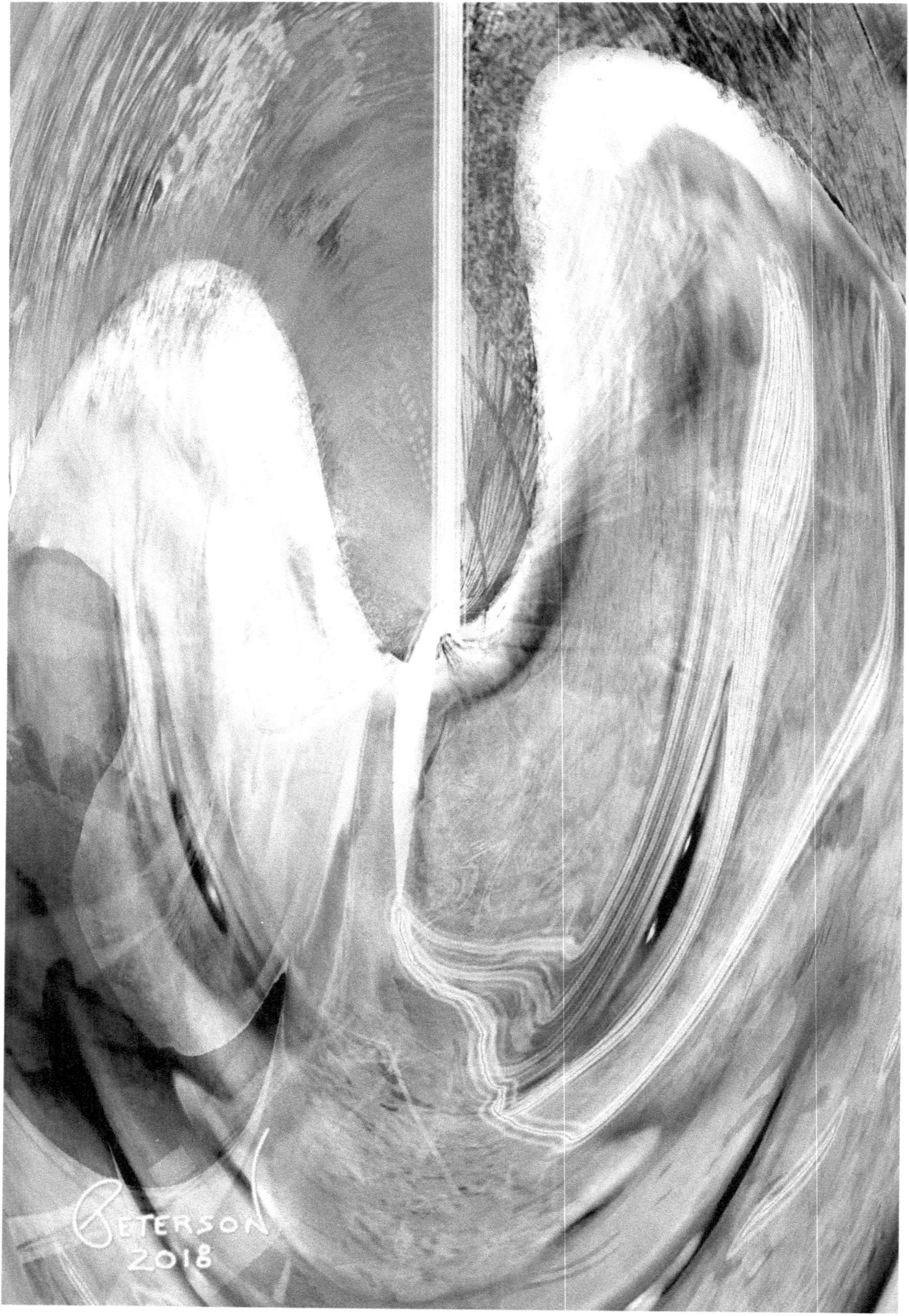
Peterson
2018

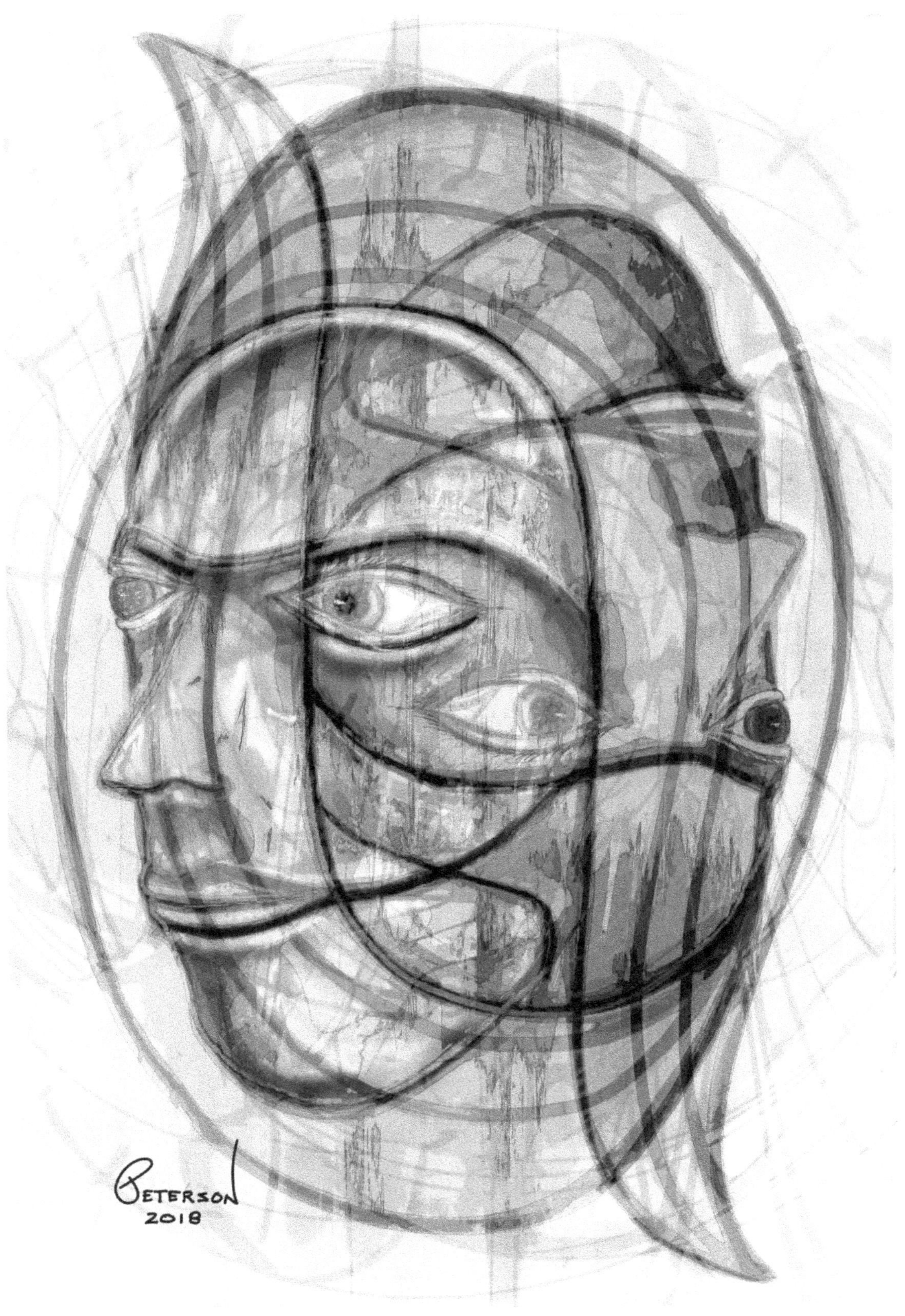

Peterson
2018

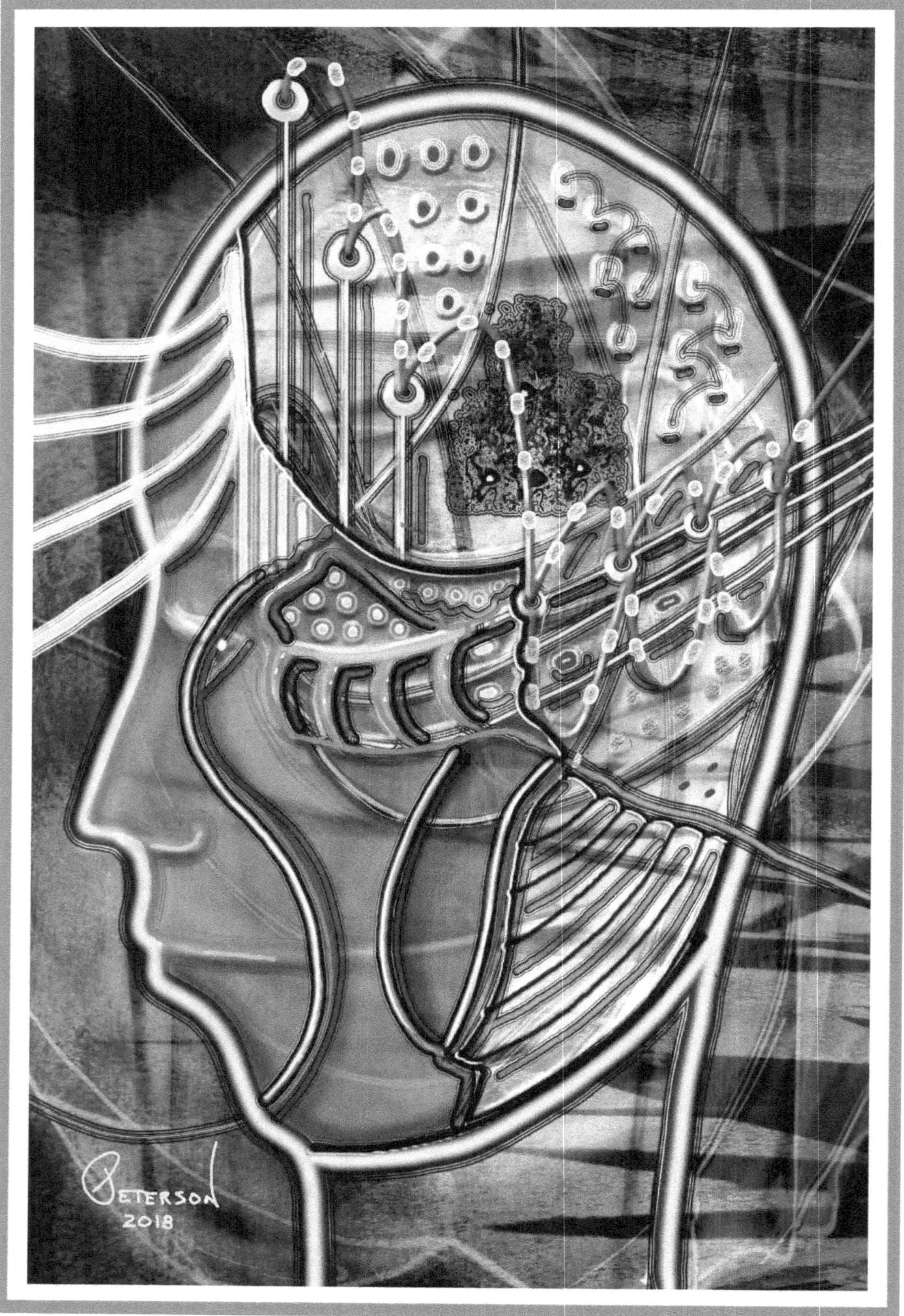

Peterson
2018

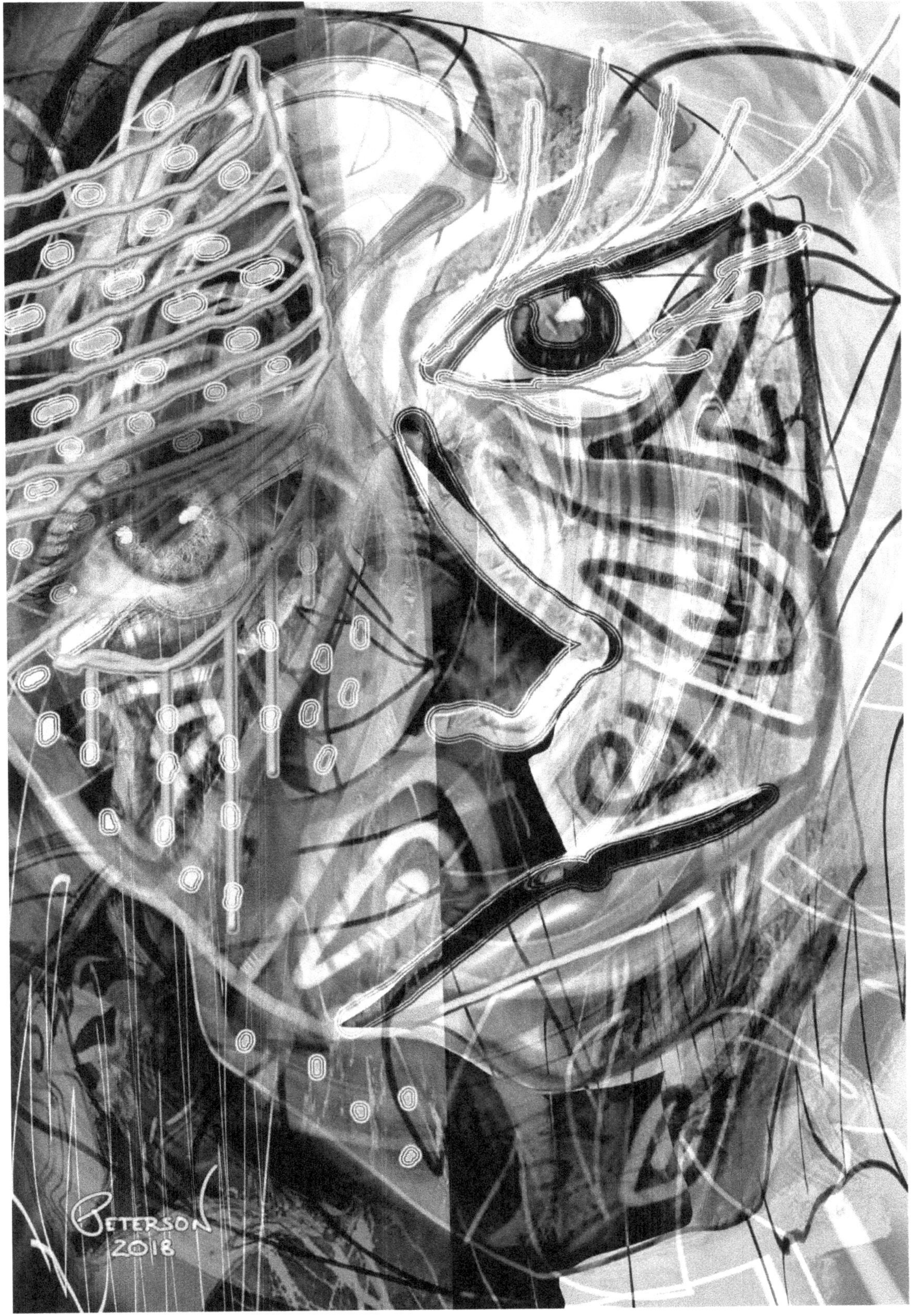

9

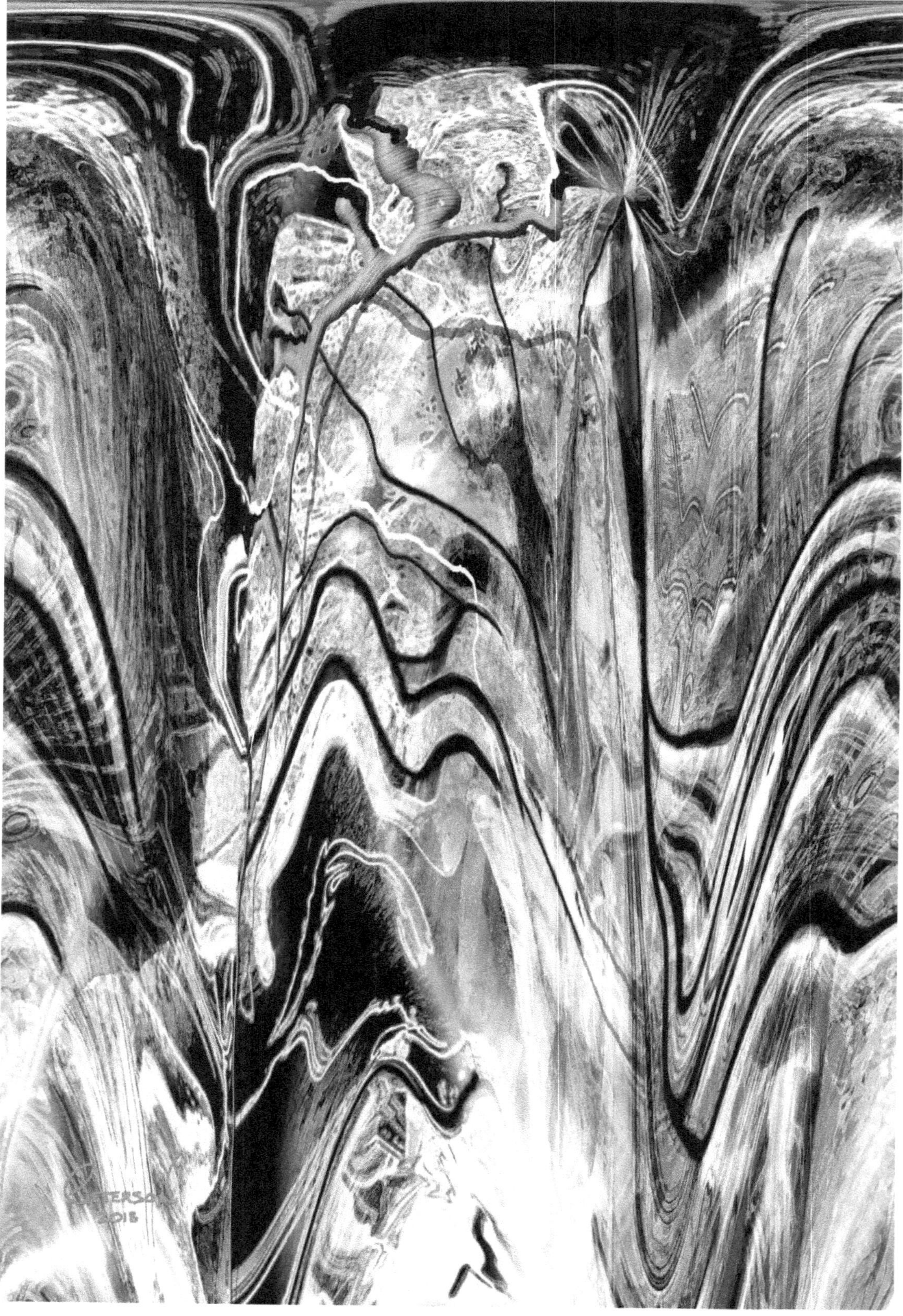

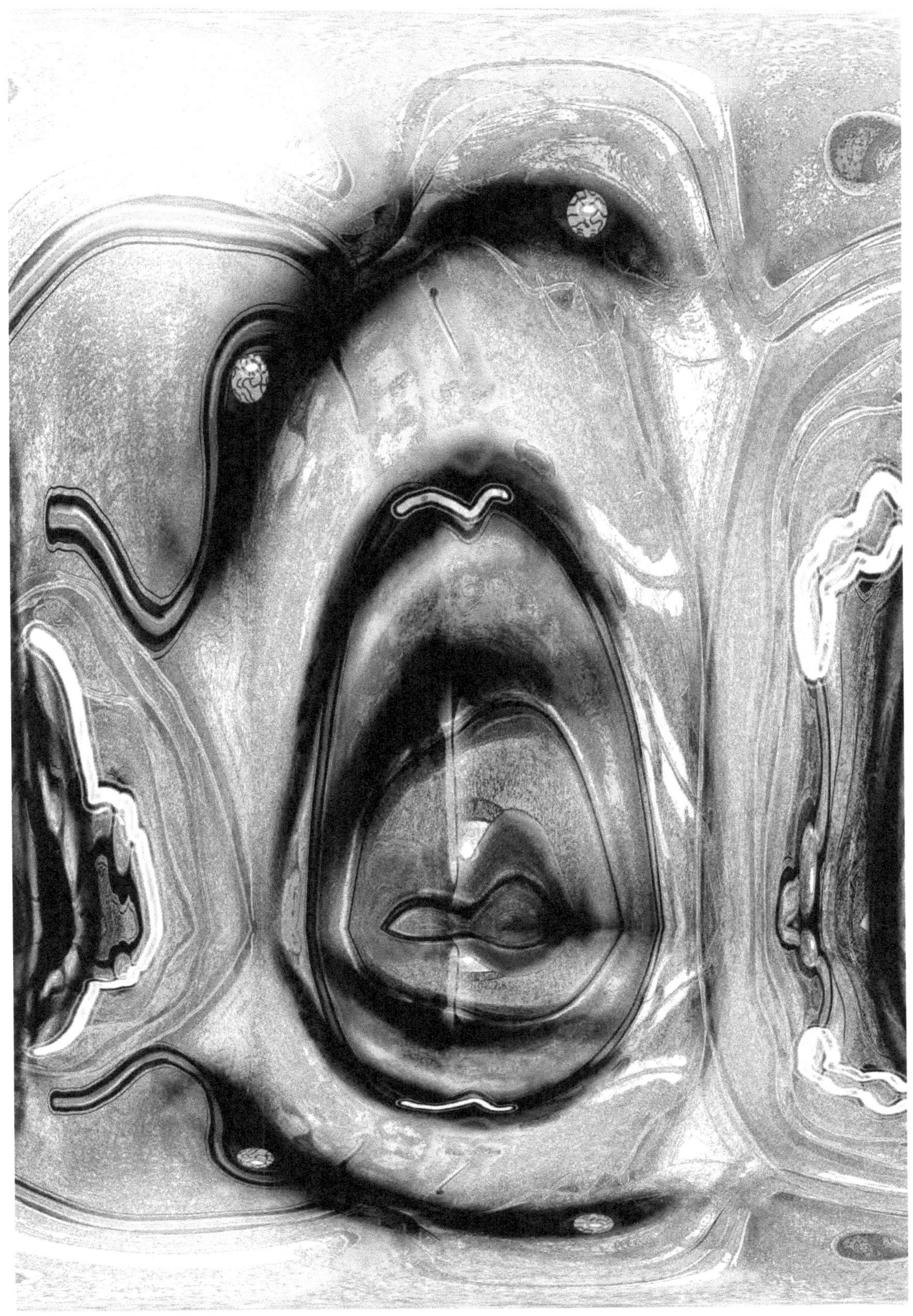

11

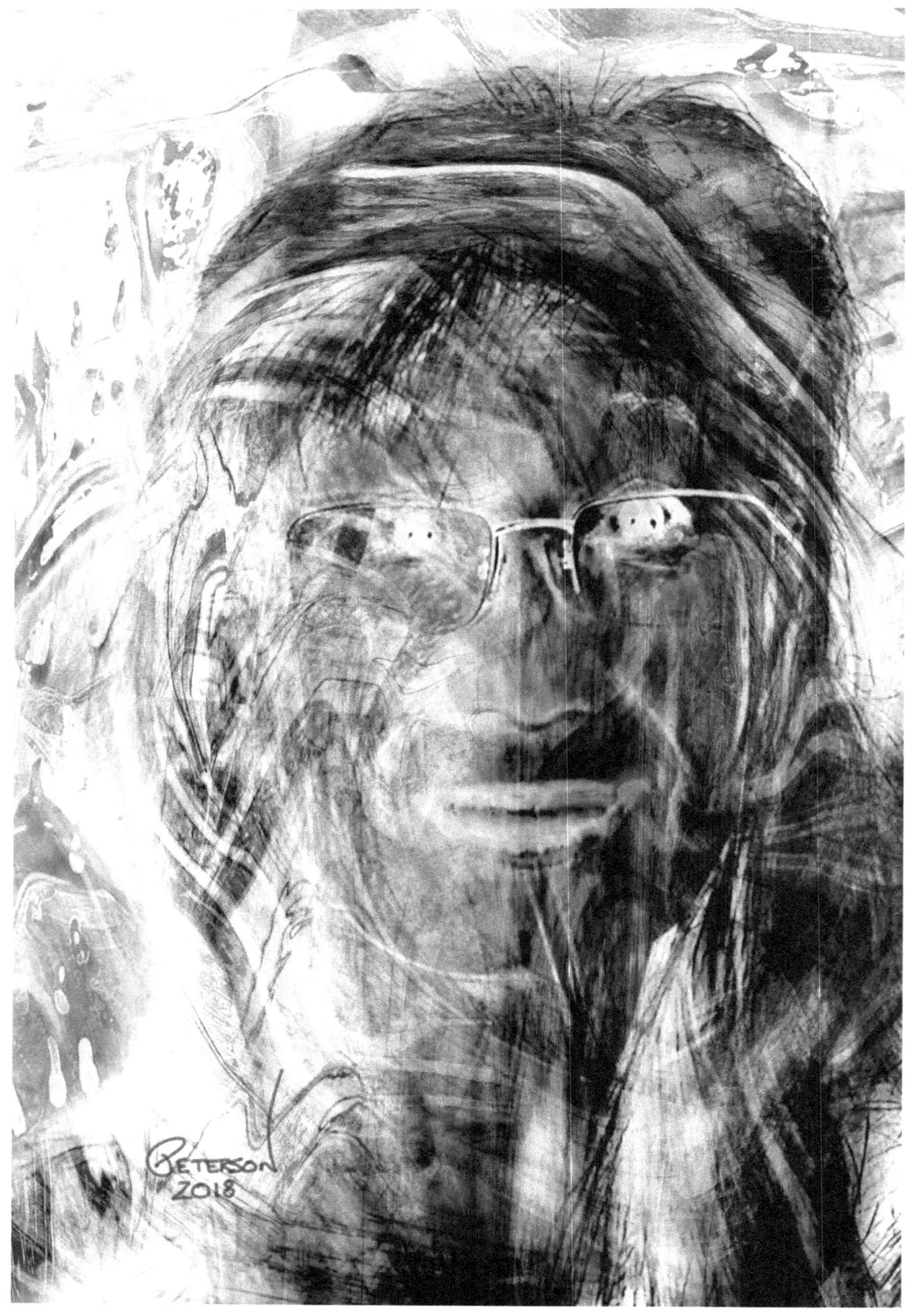

Peterson
2018

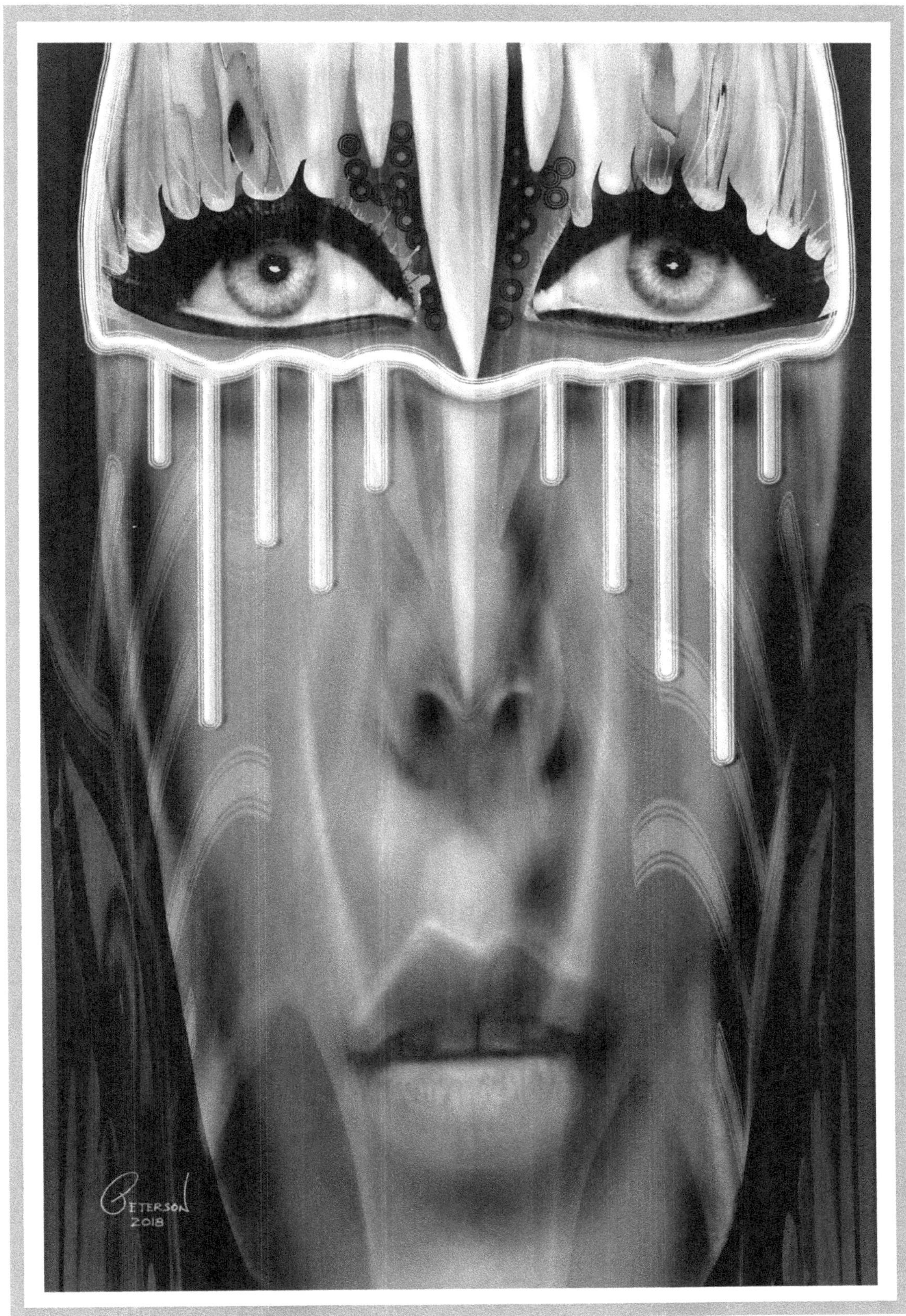
Peterson
2018

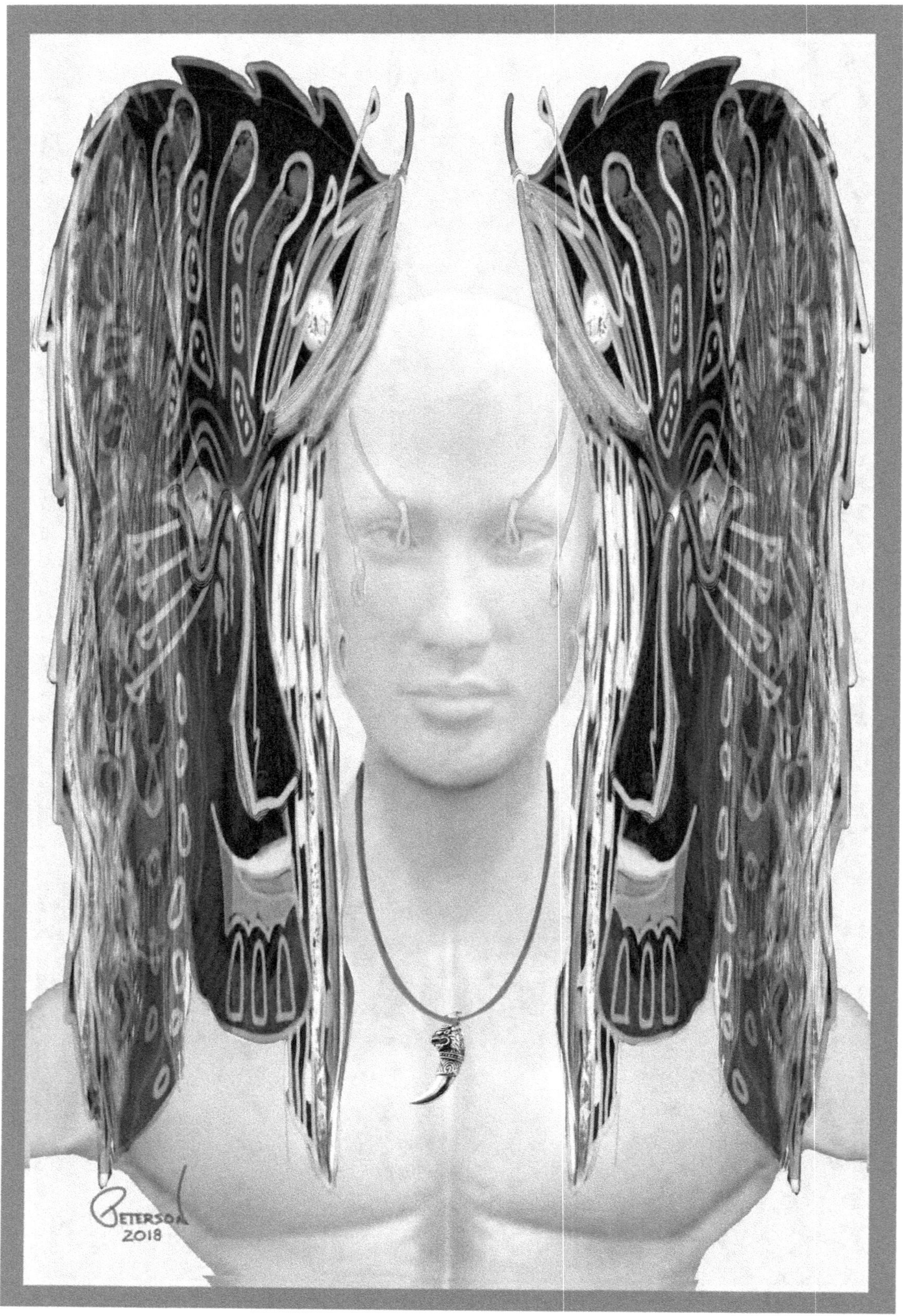

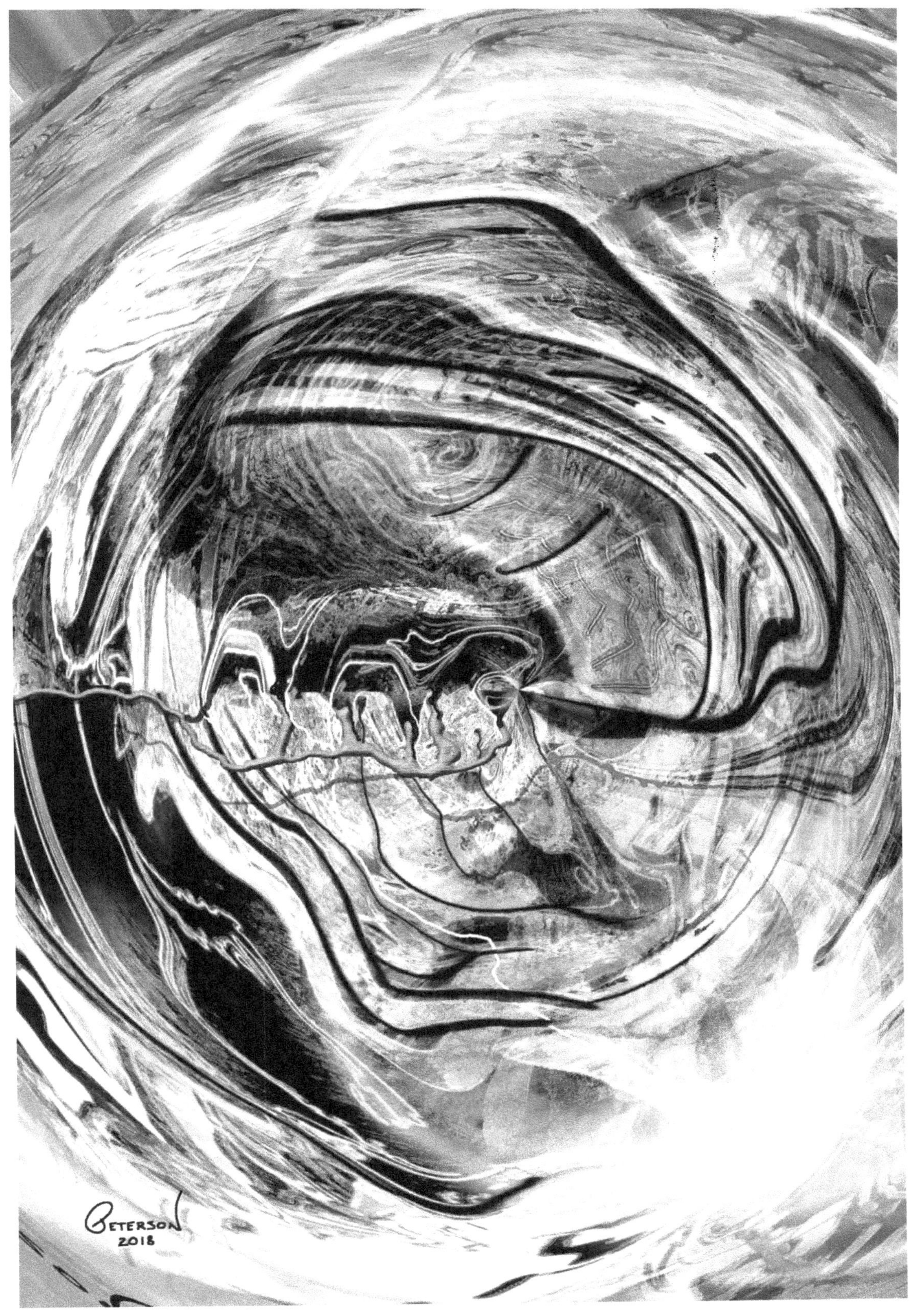

Peterson
2018

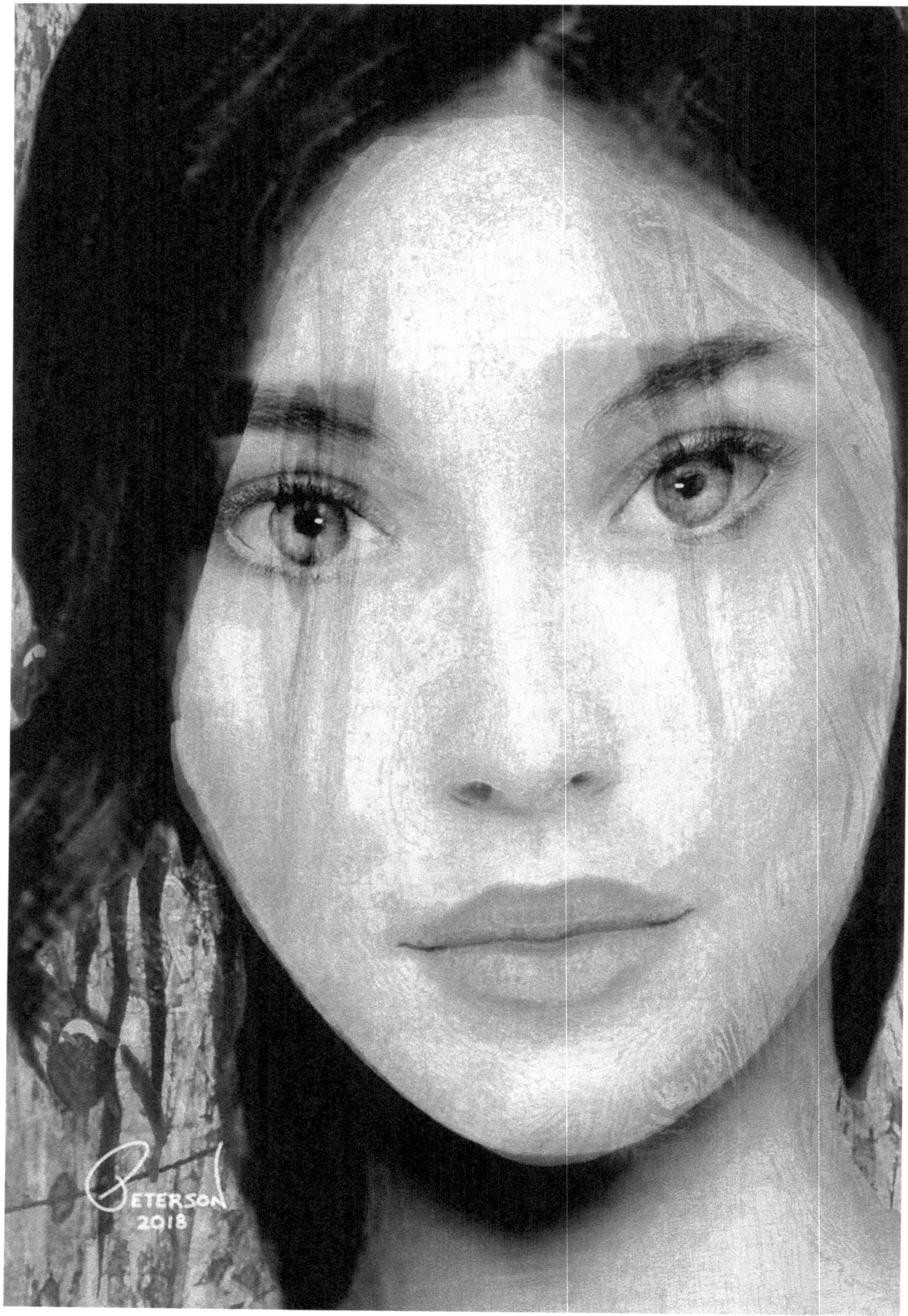
Peterson
2018

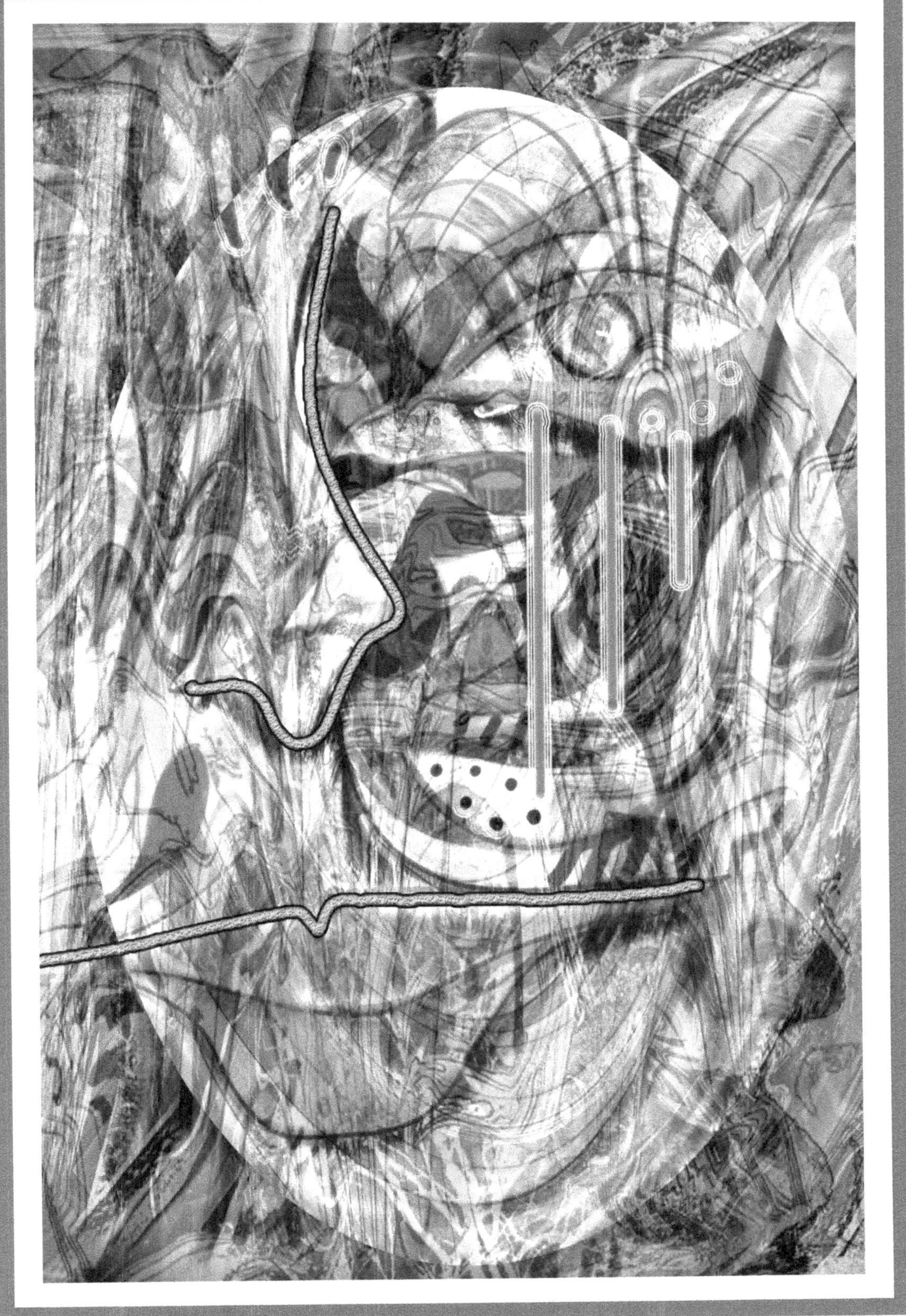

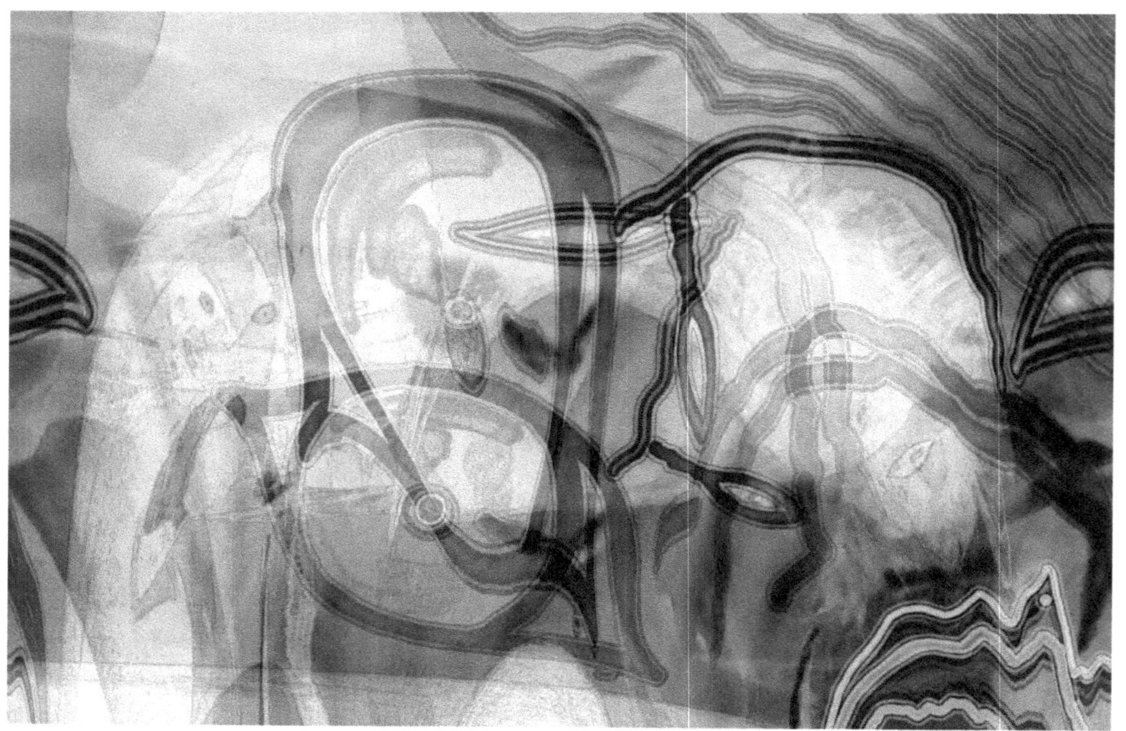

18

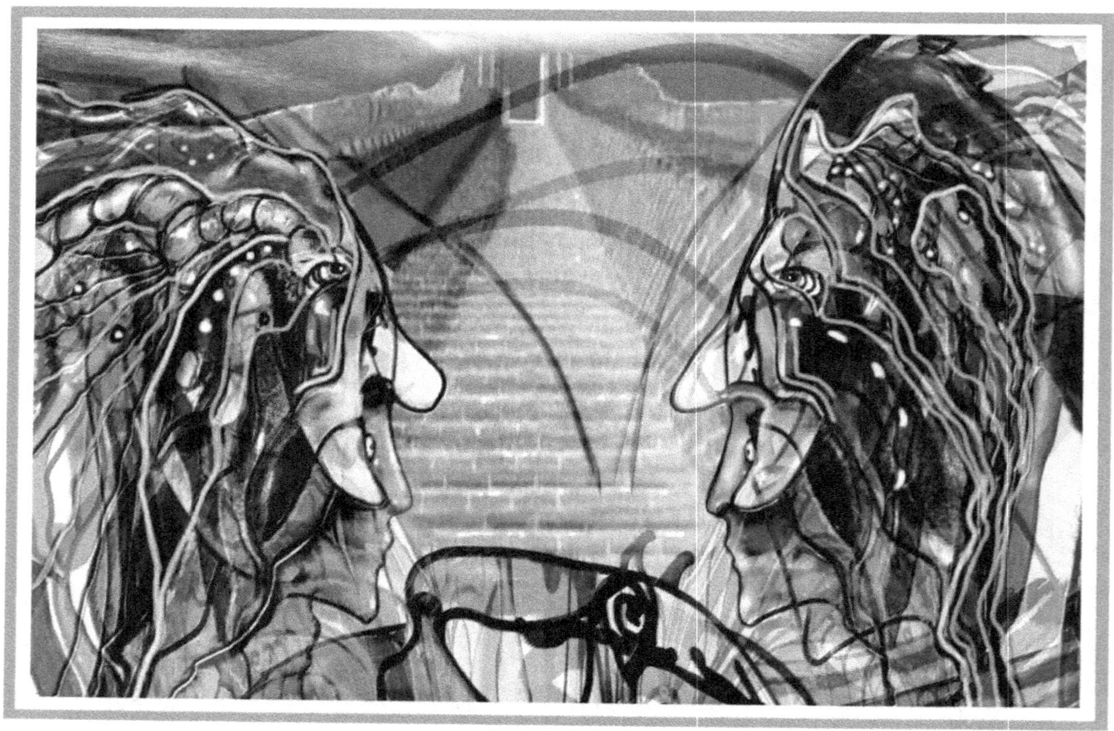

19

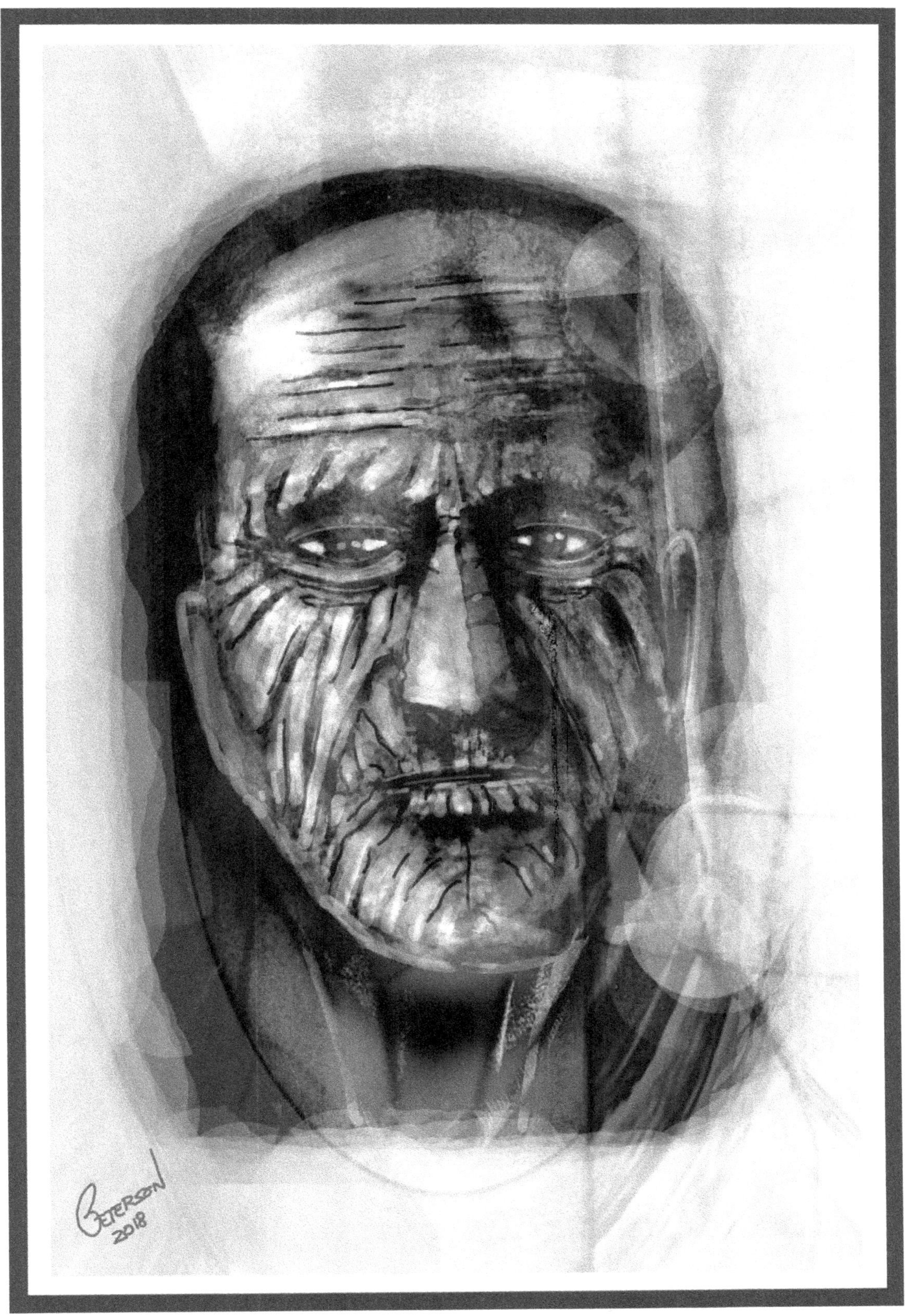
Peterson
2018

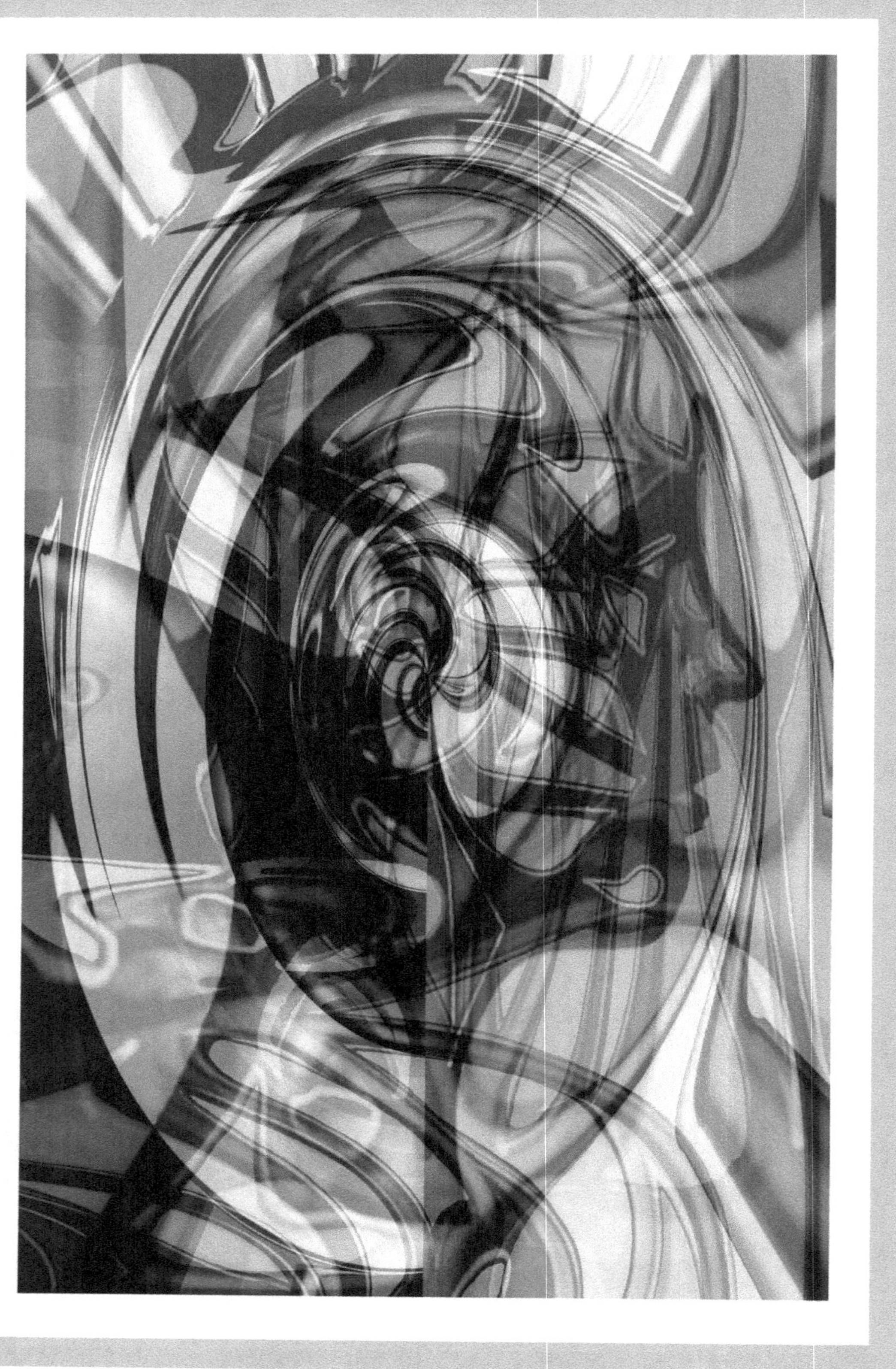

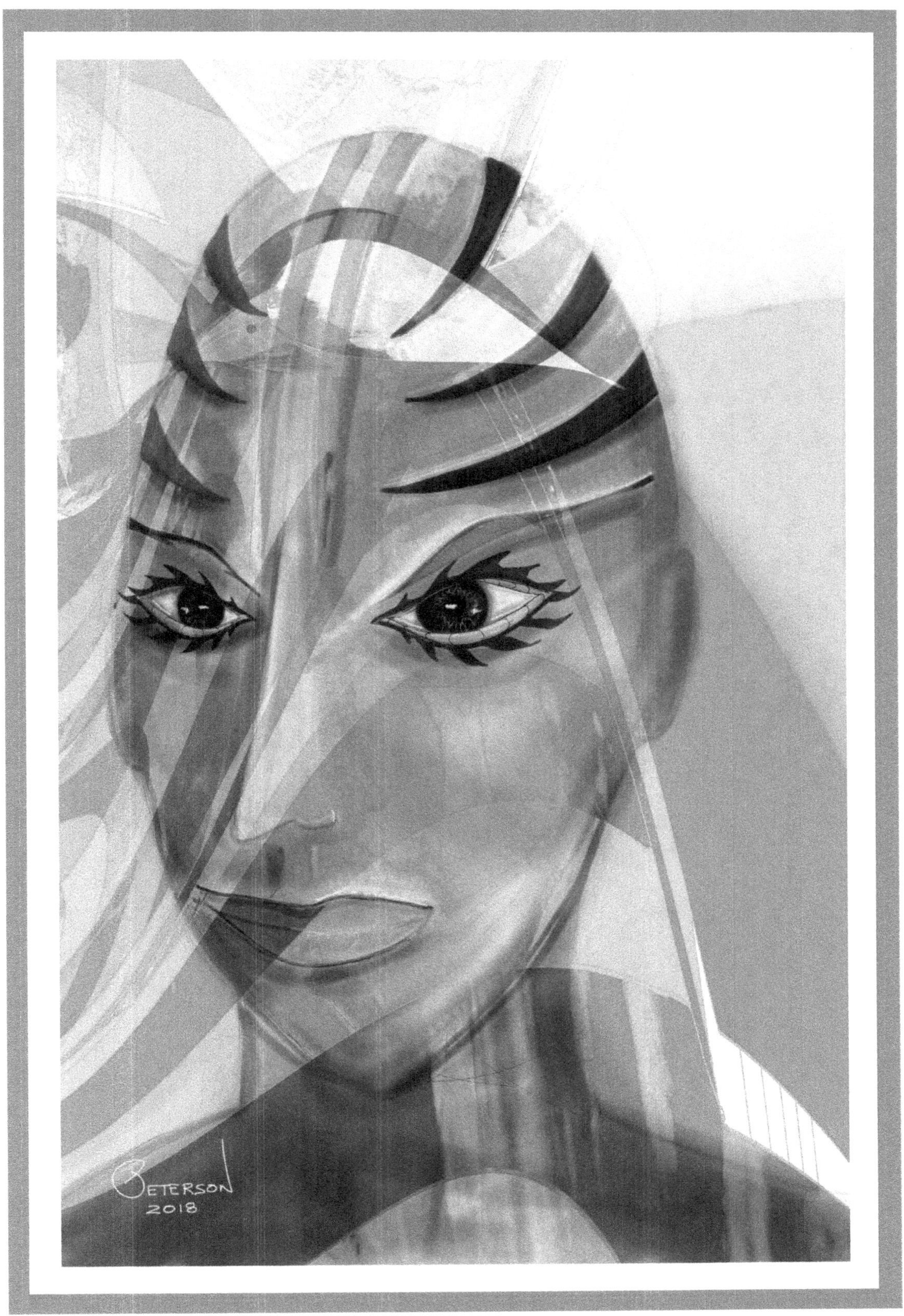
PETERSON
2018

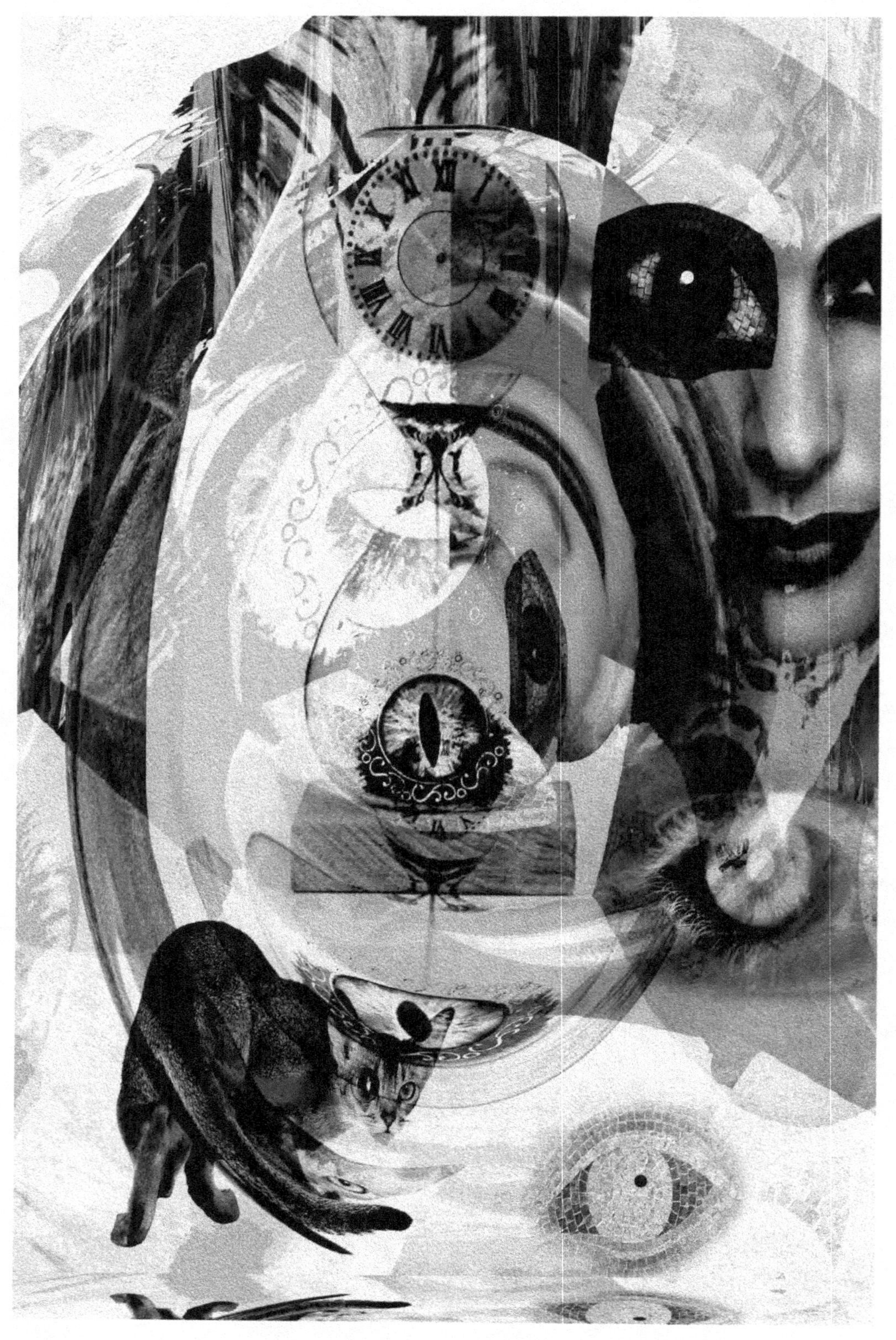

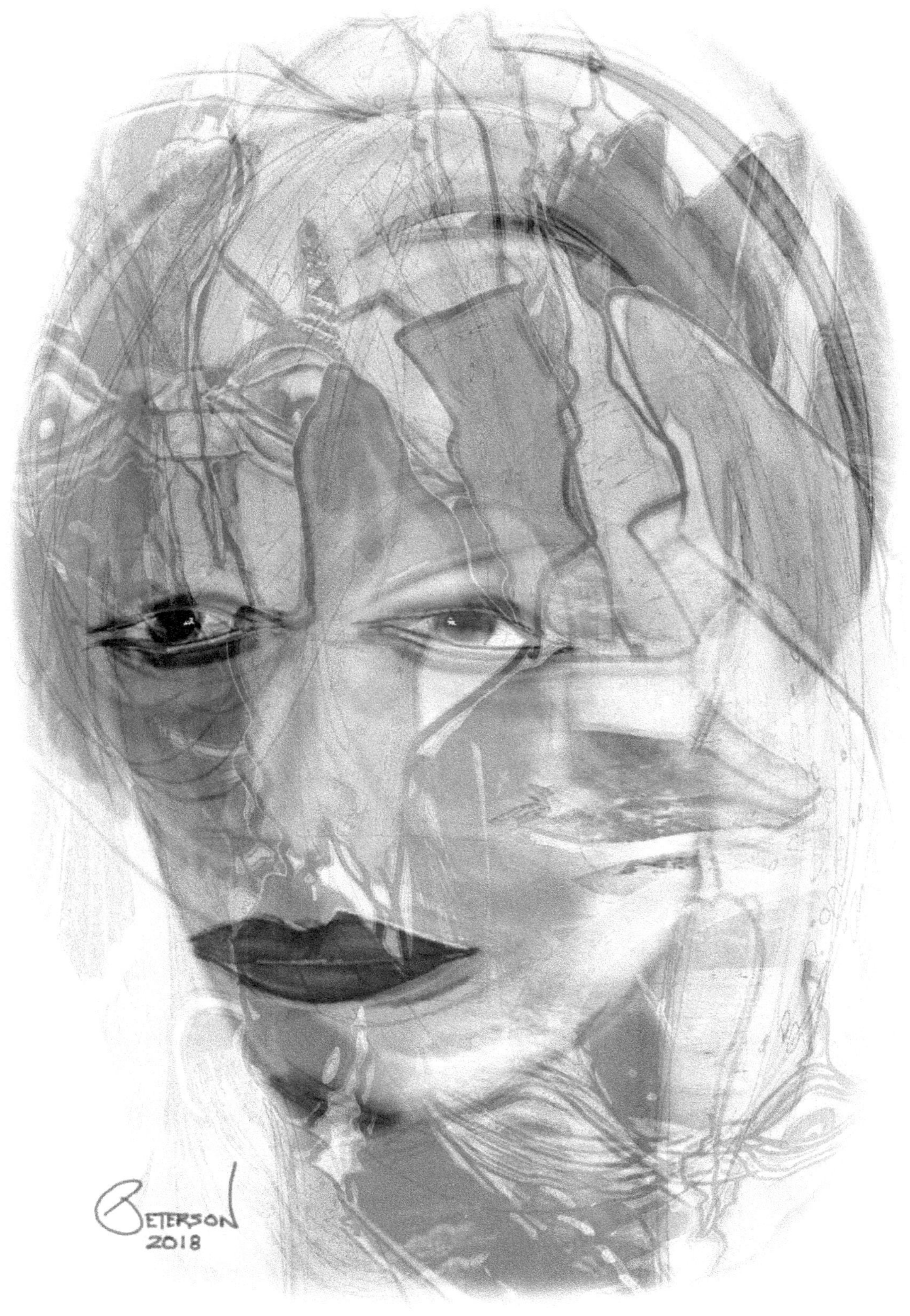

Peterson
2018

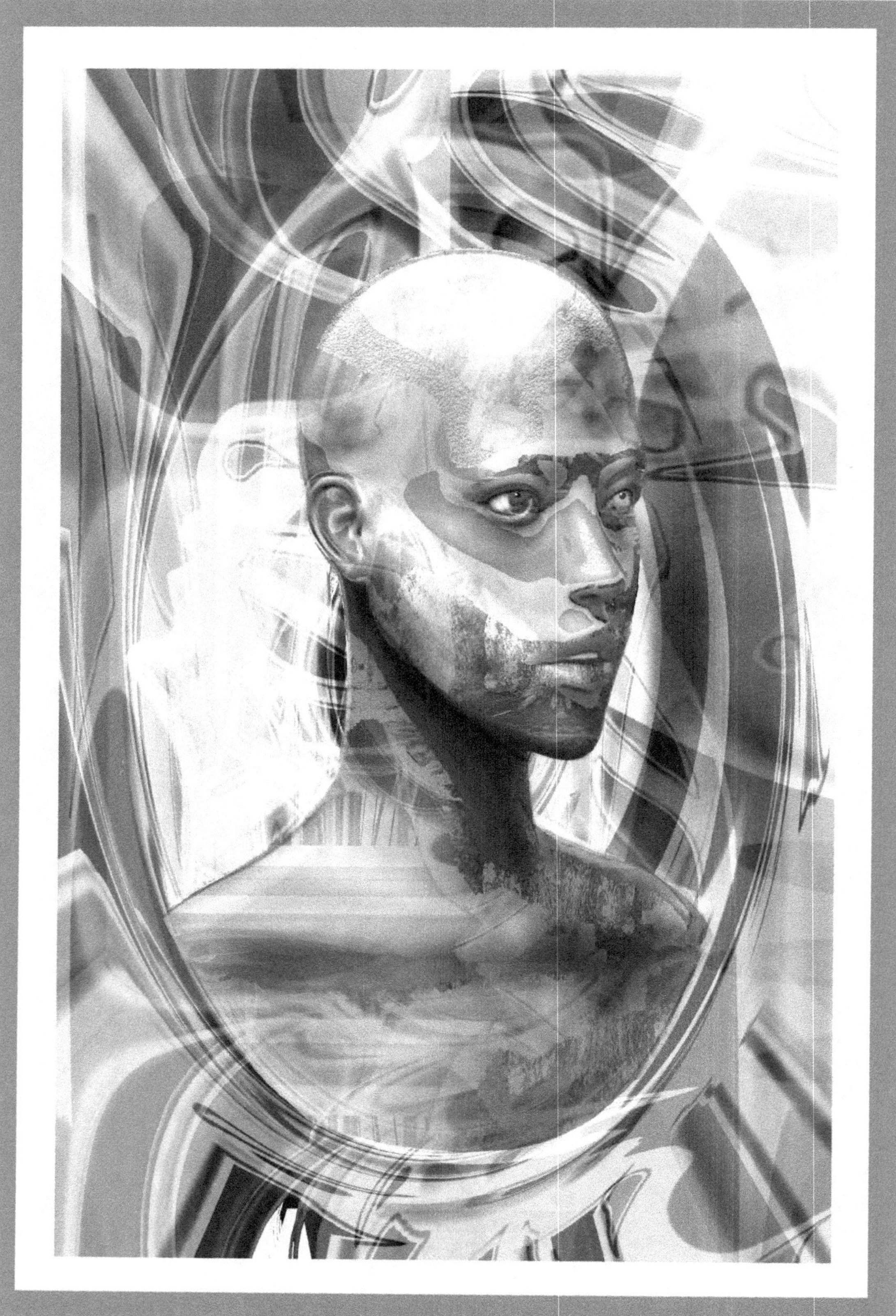

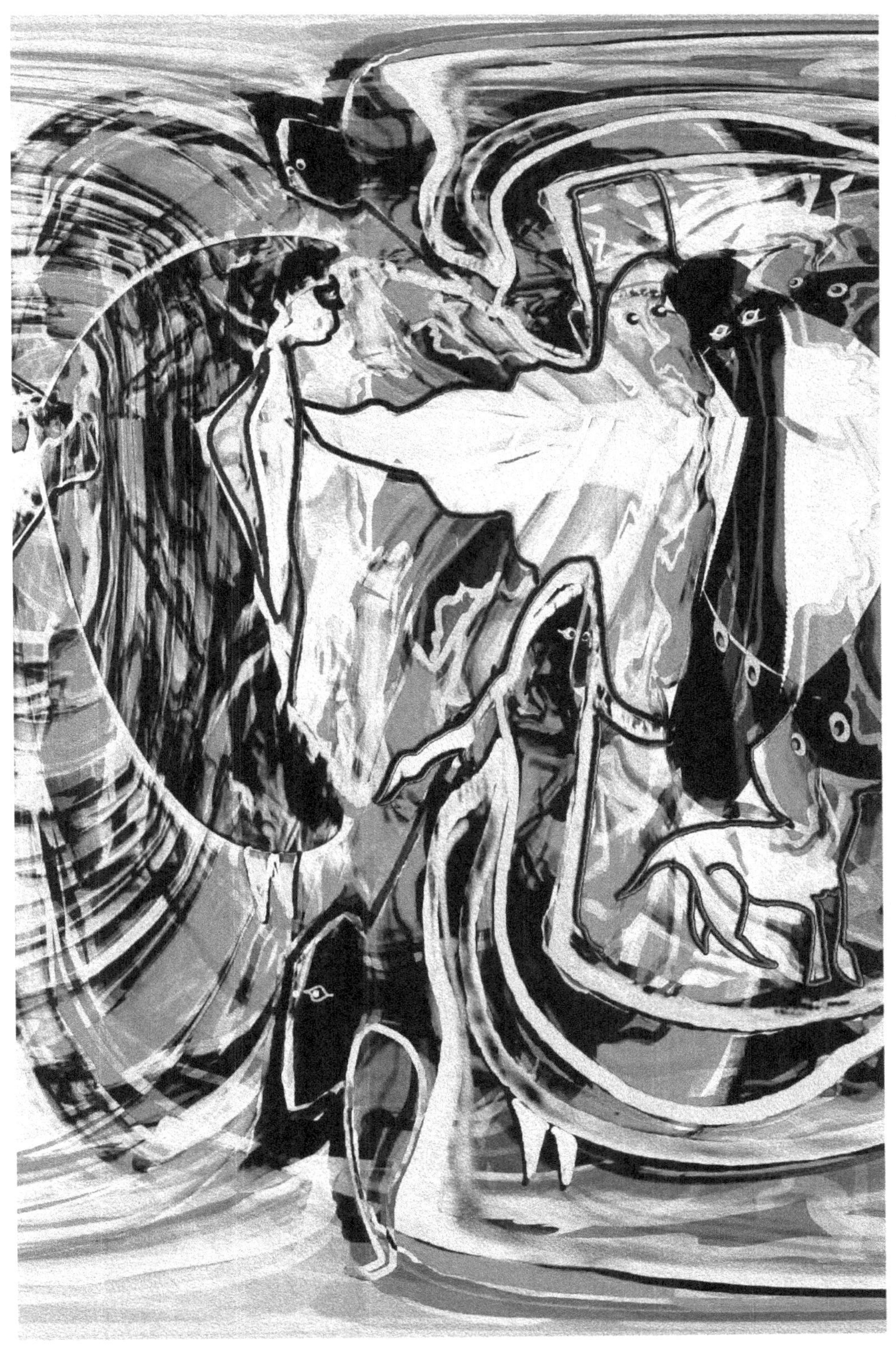

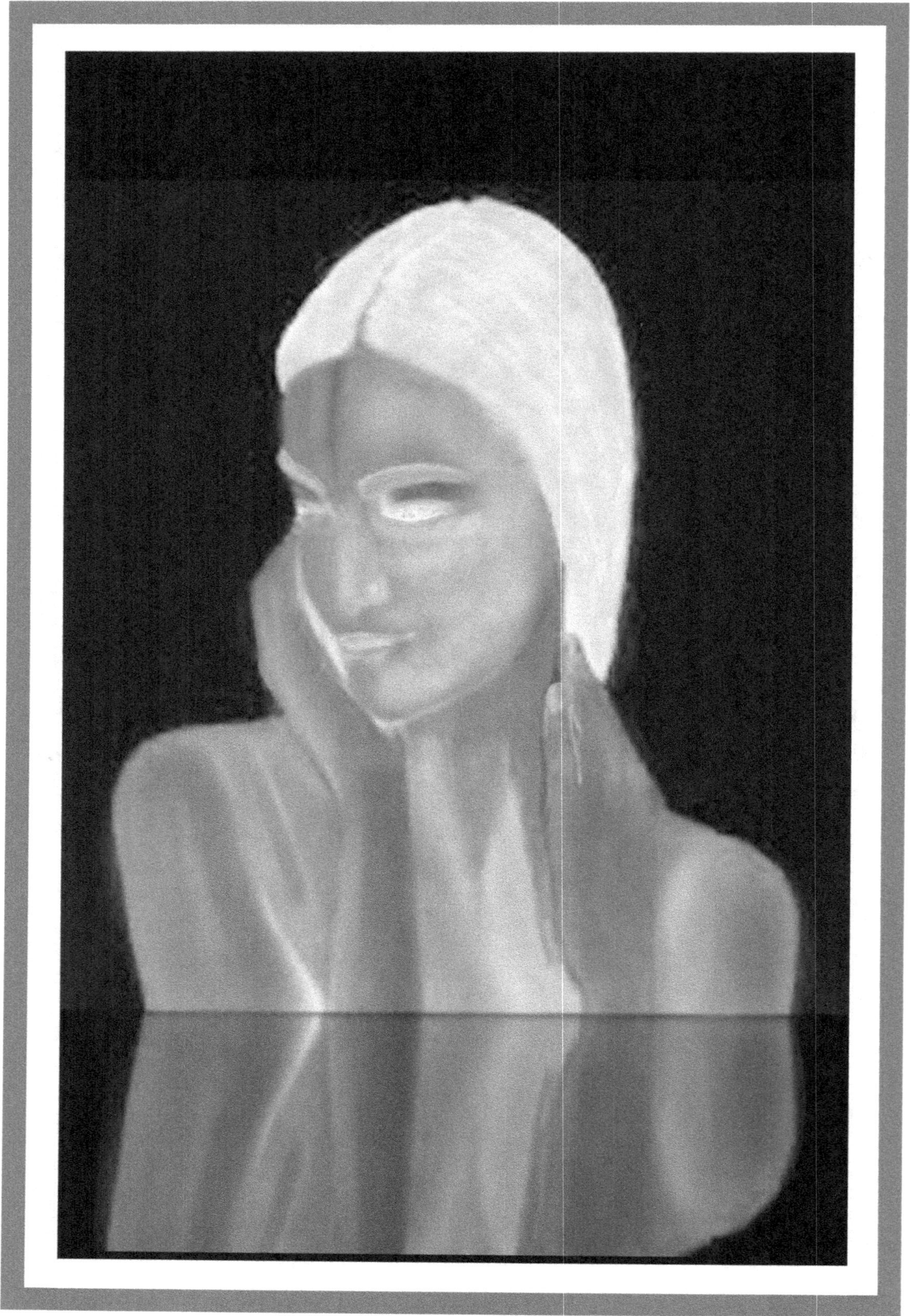

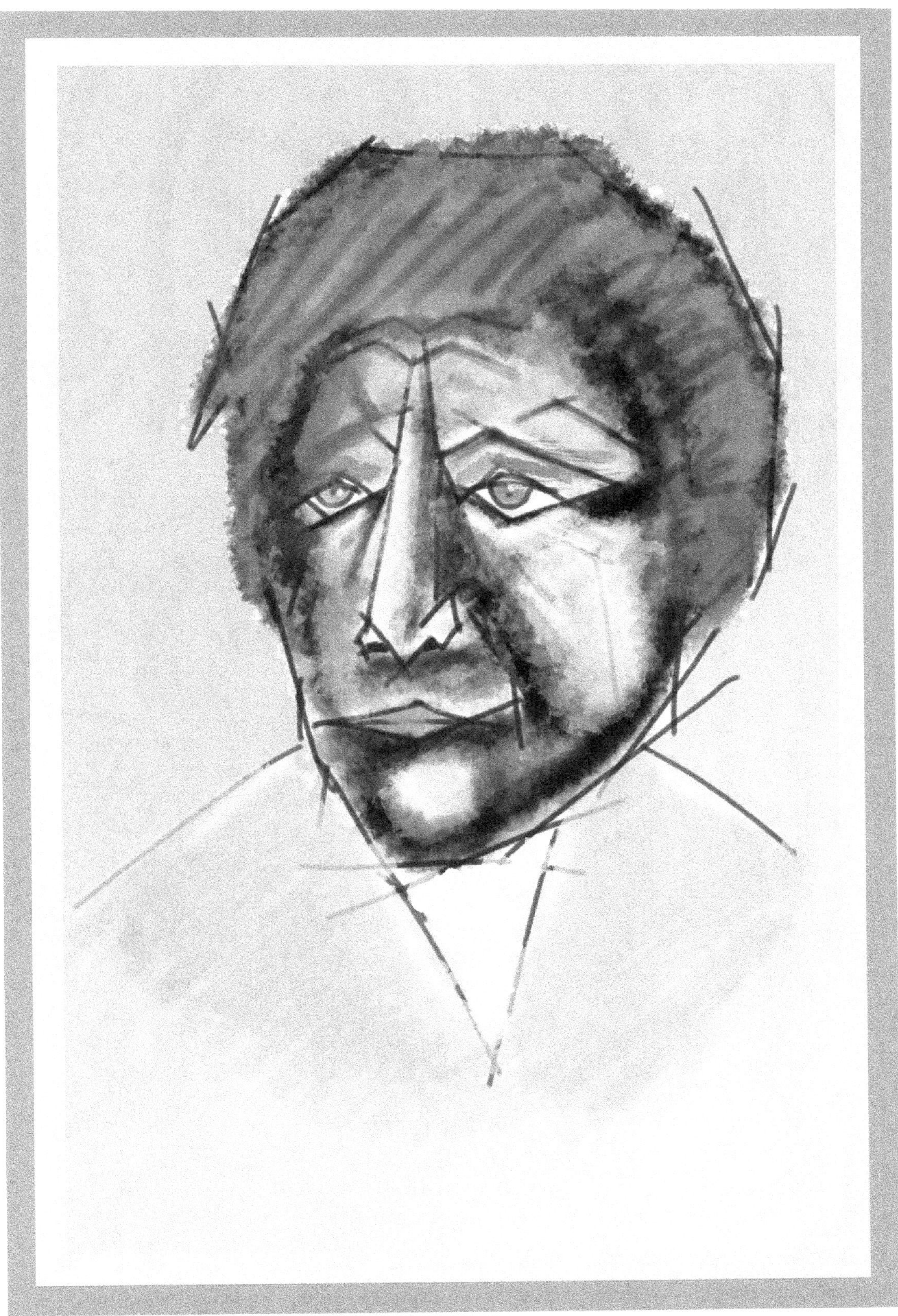

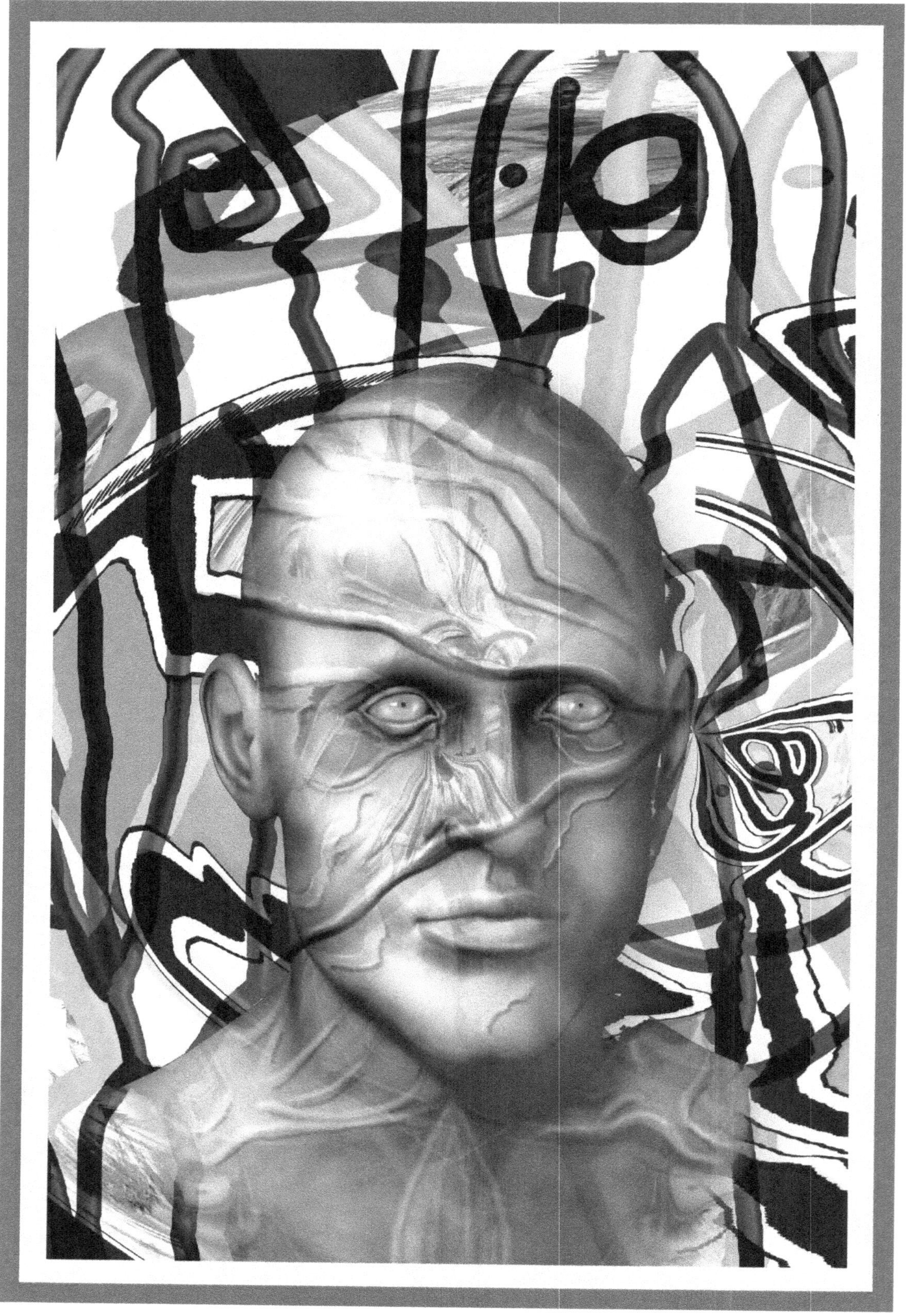

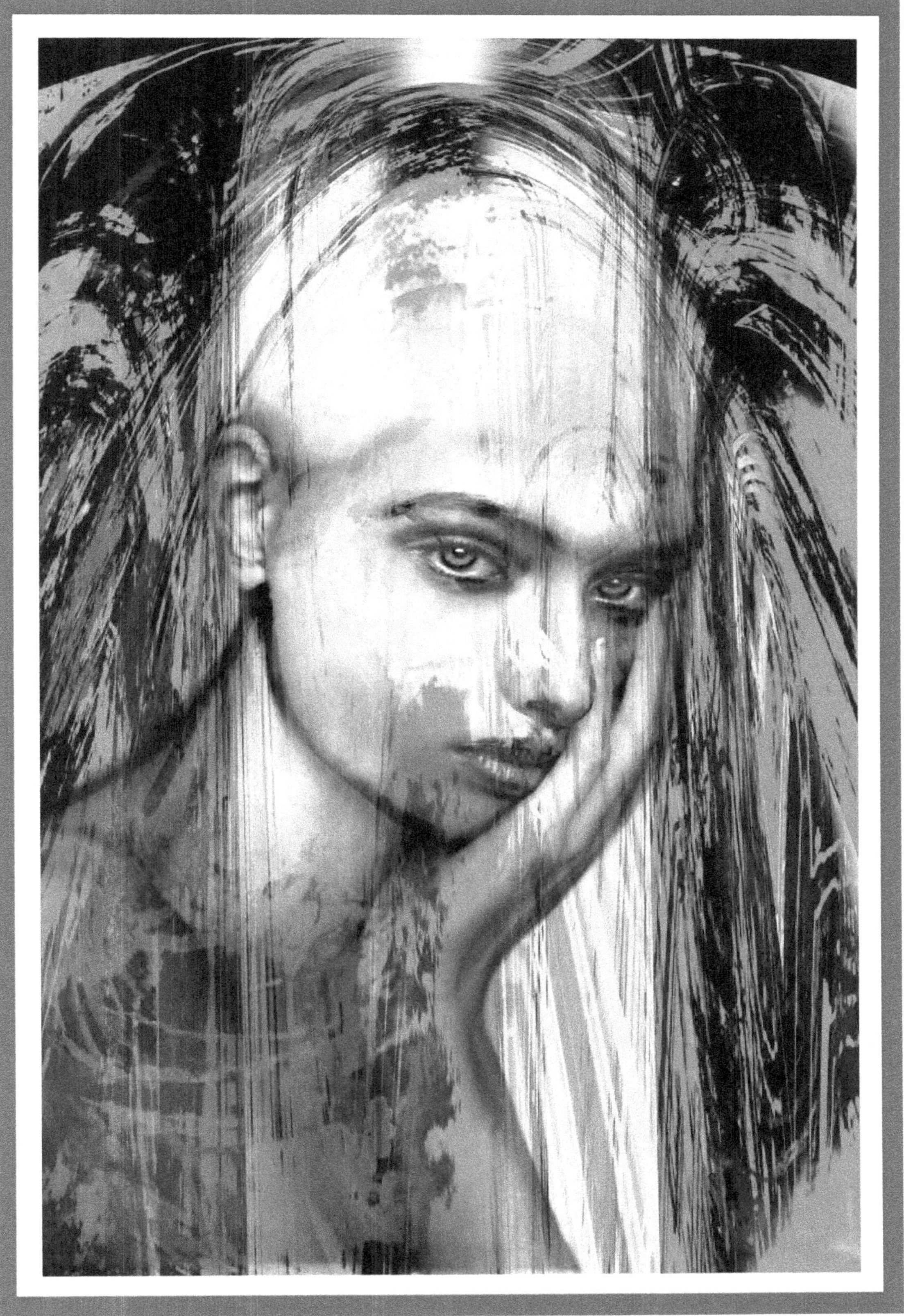

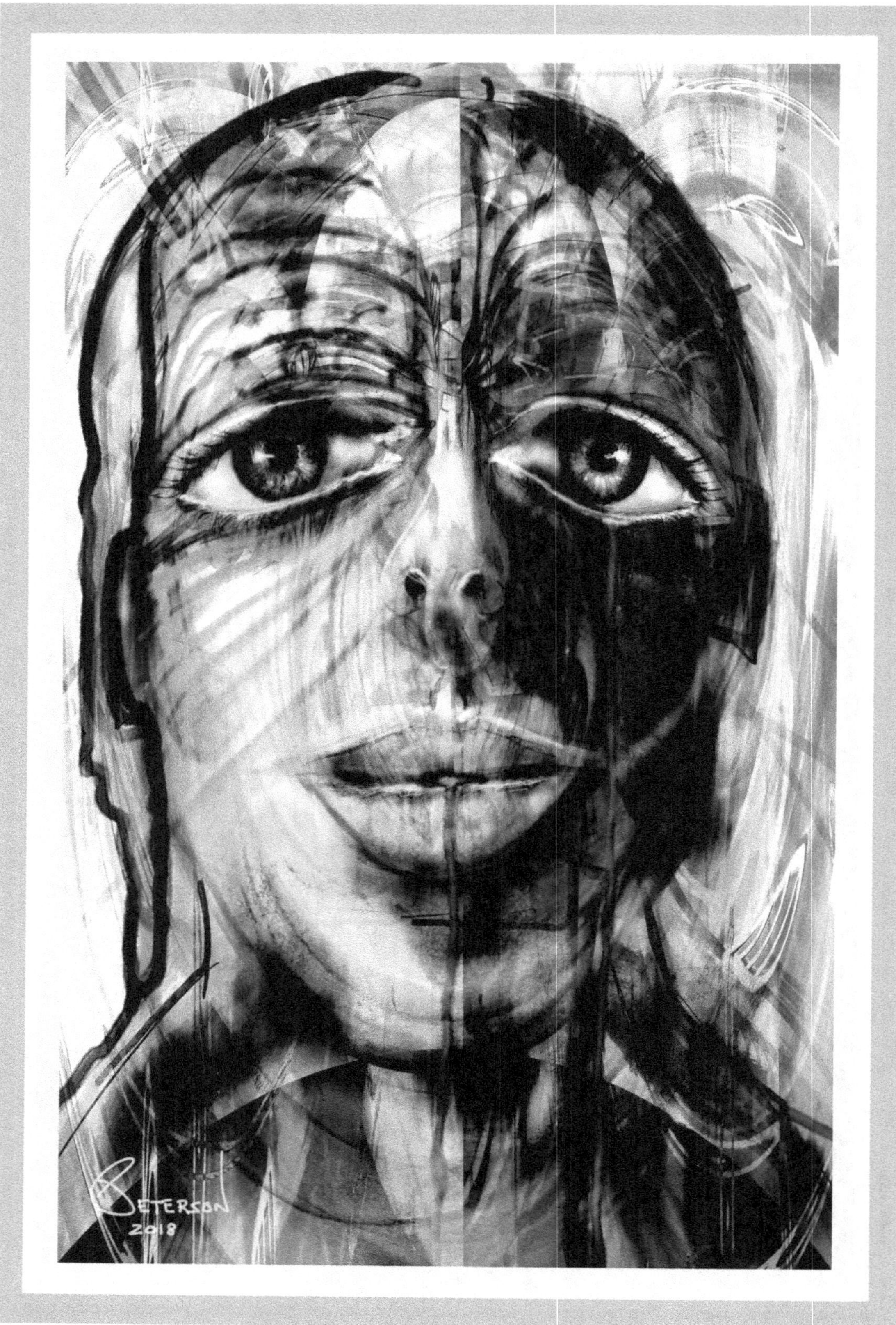

PETERSON
2018

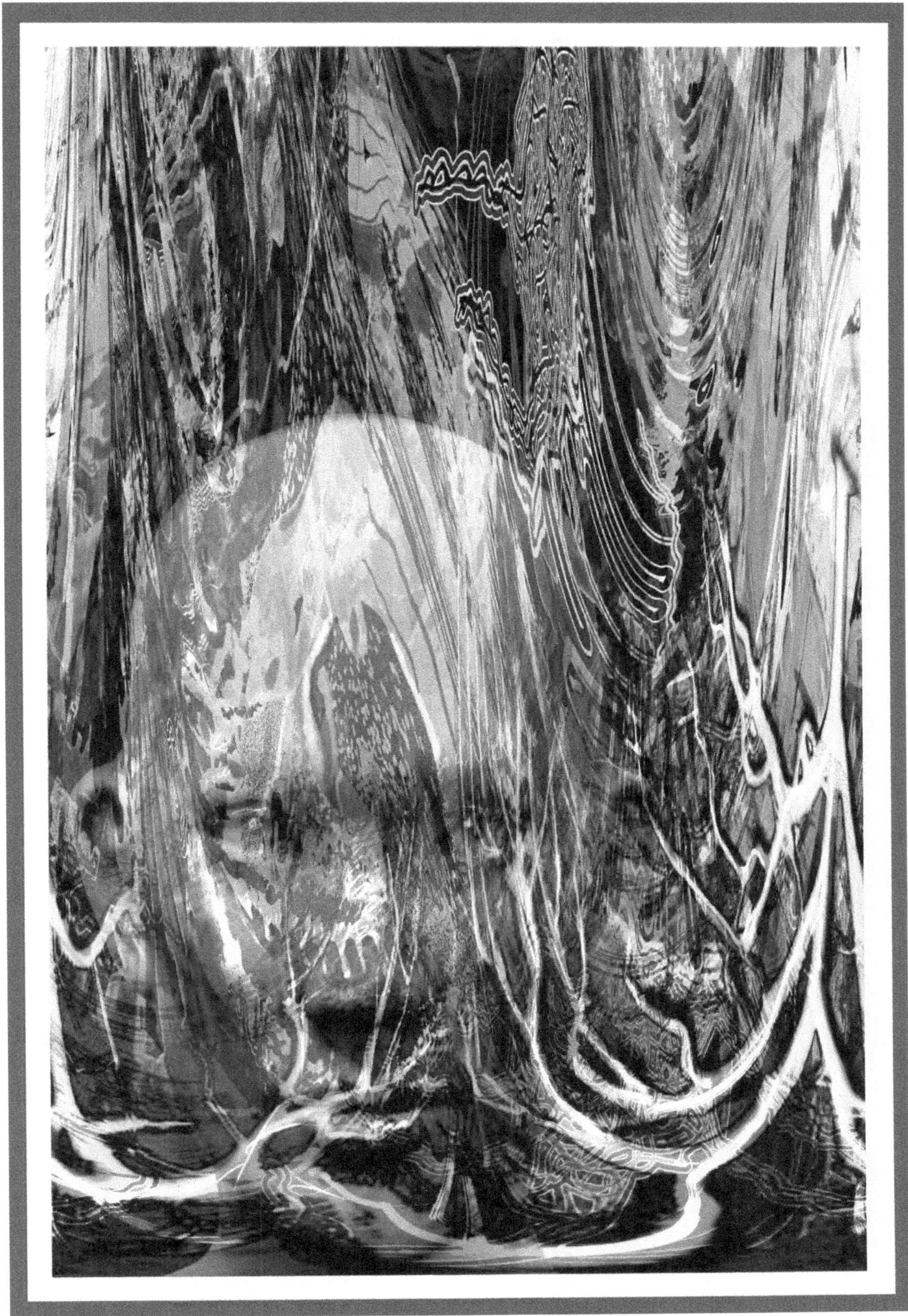

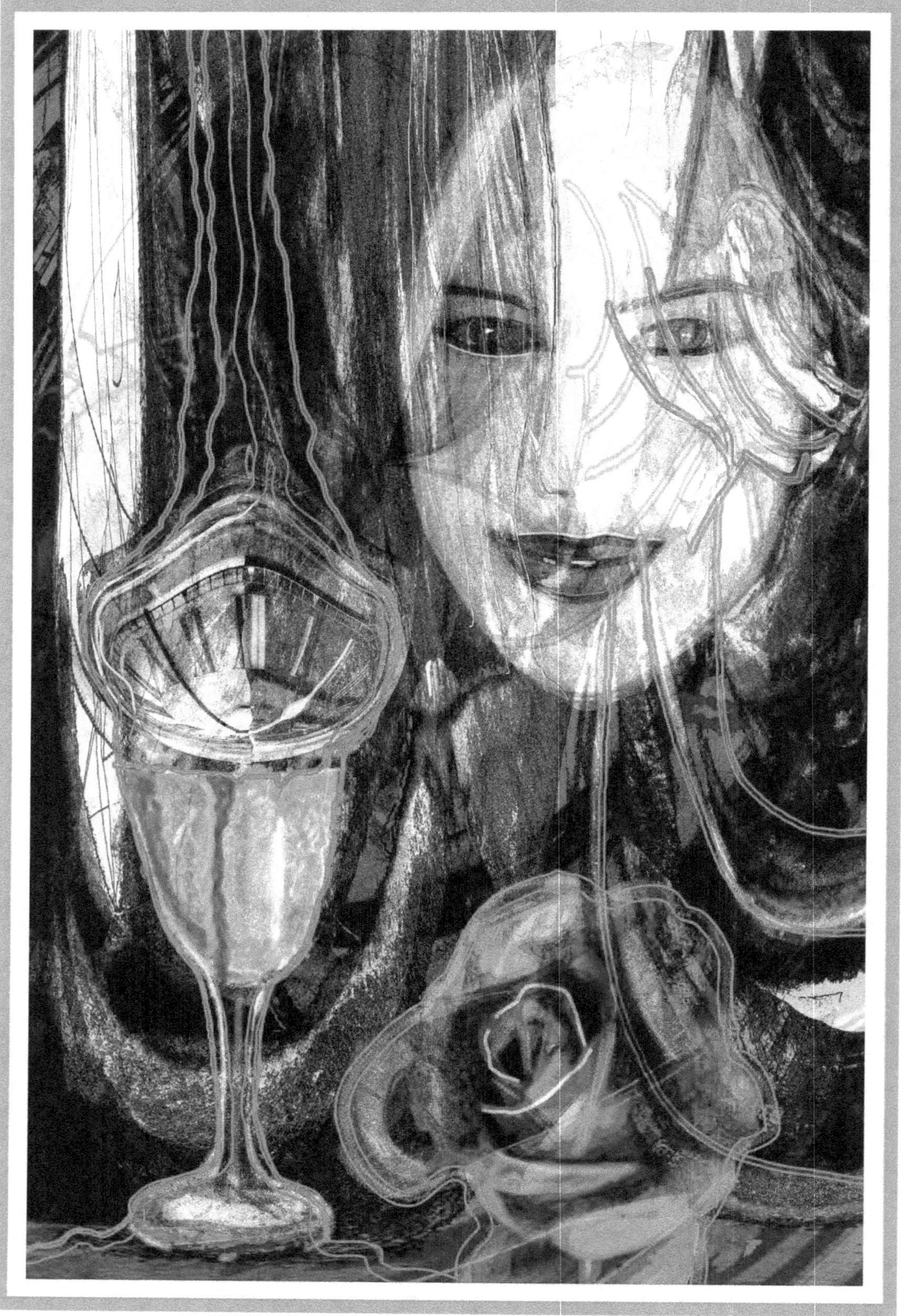

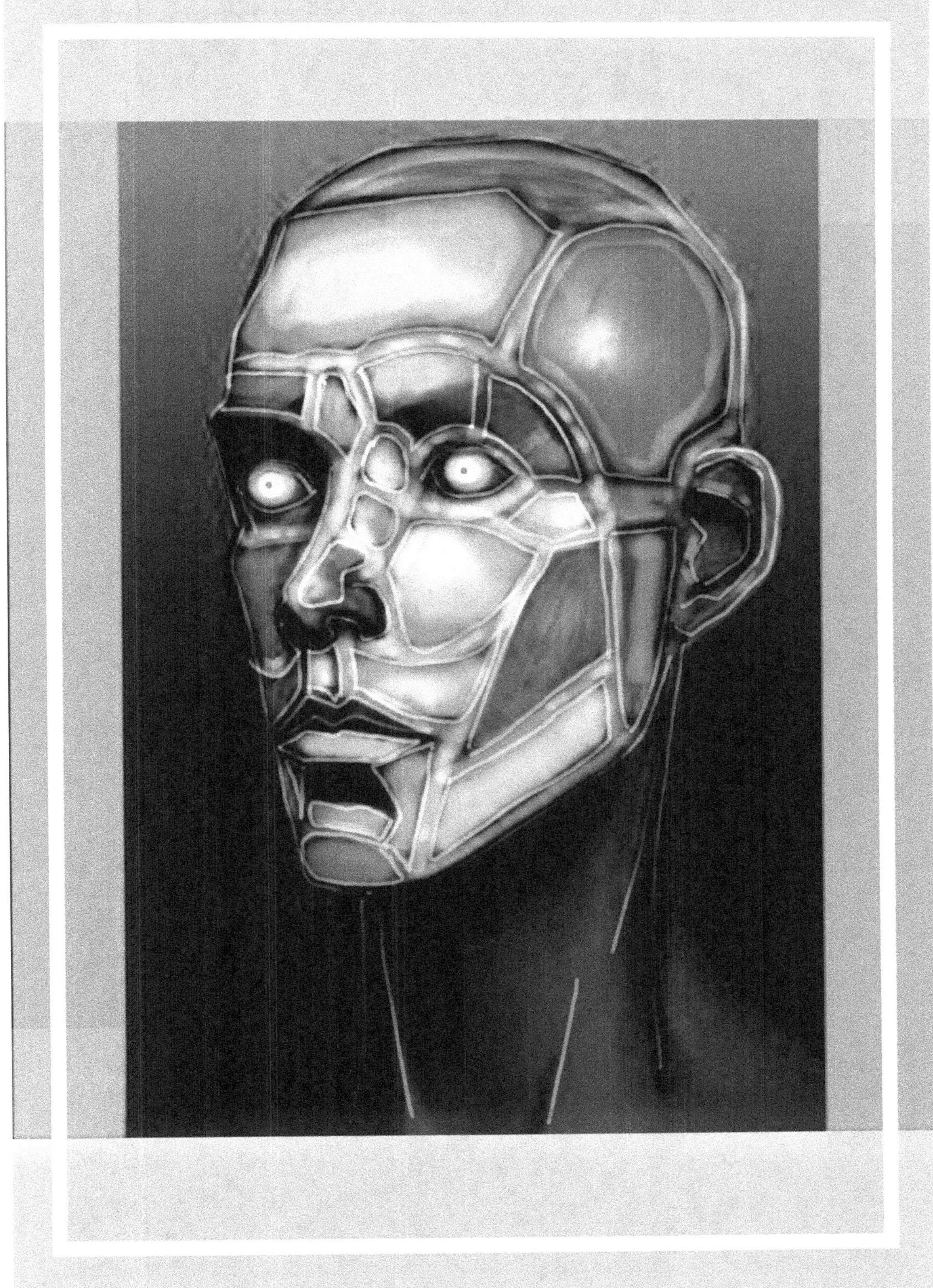

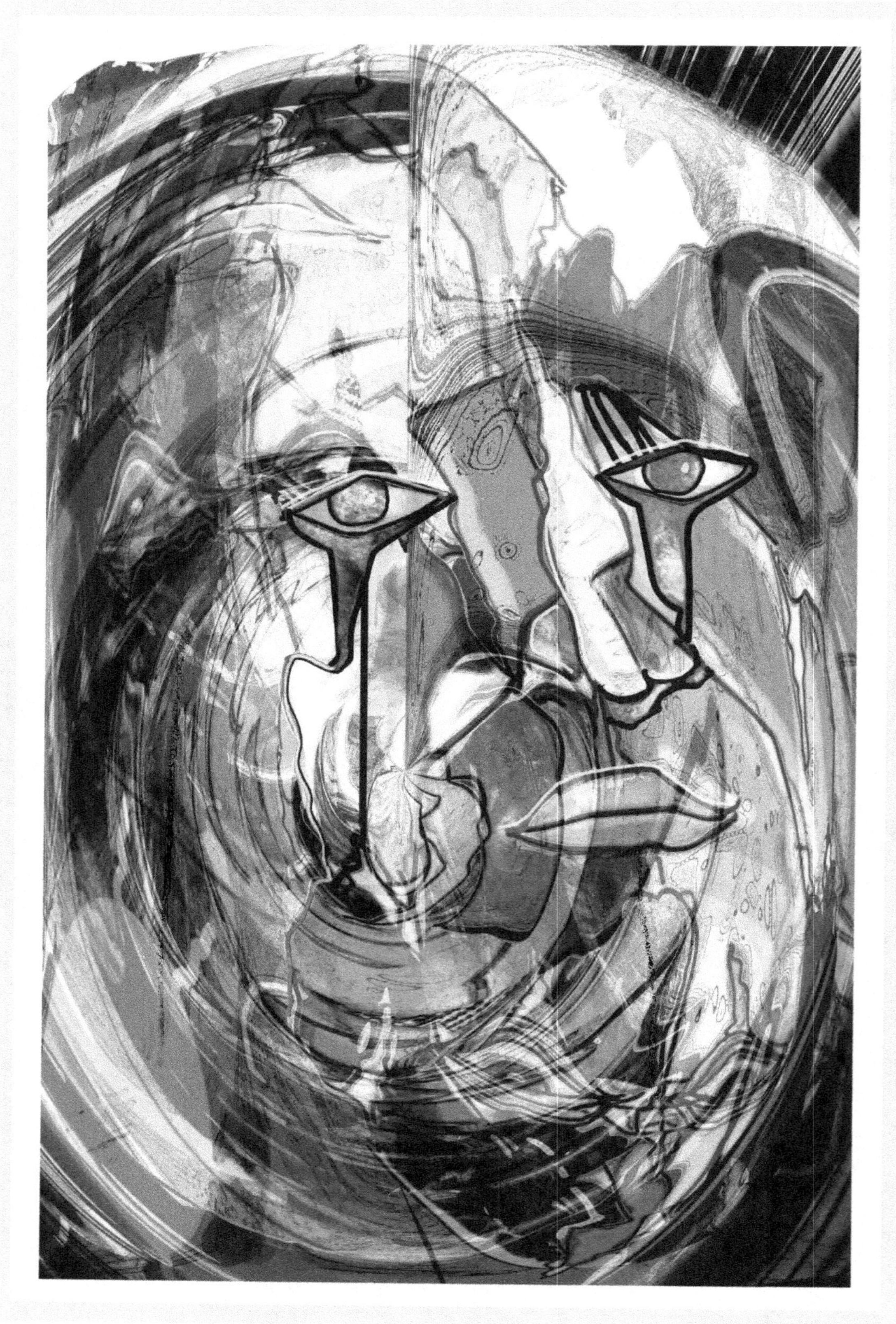

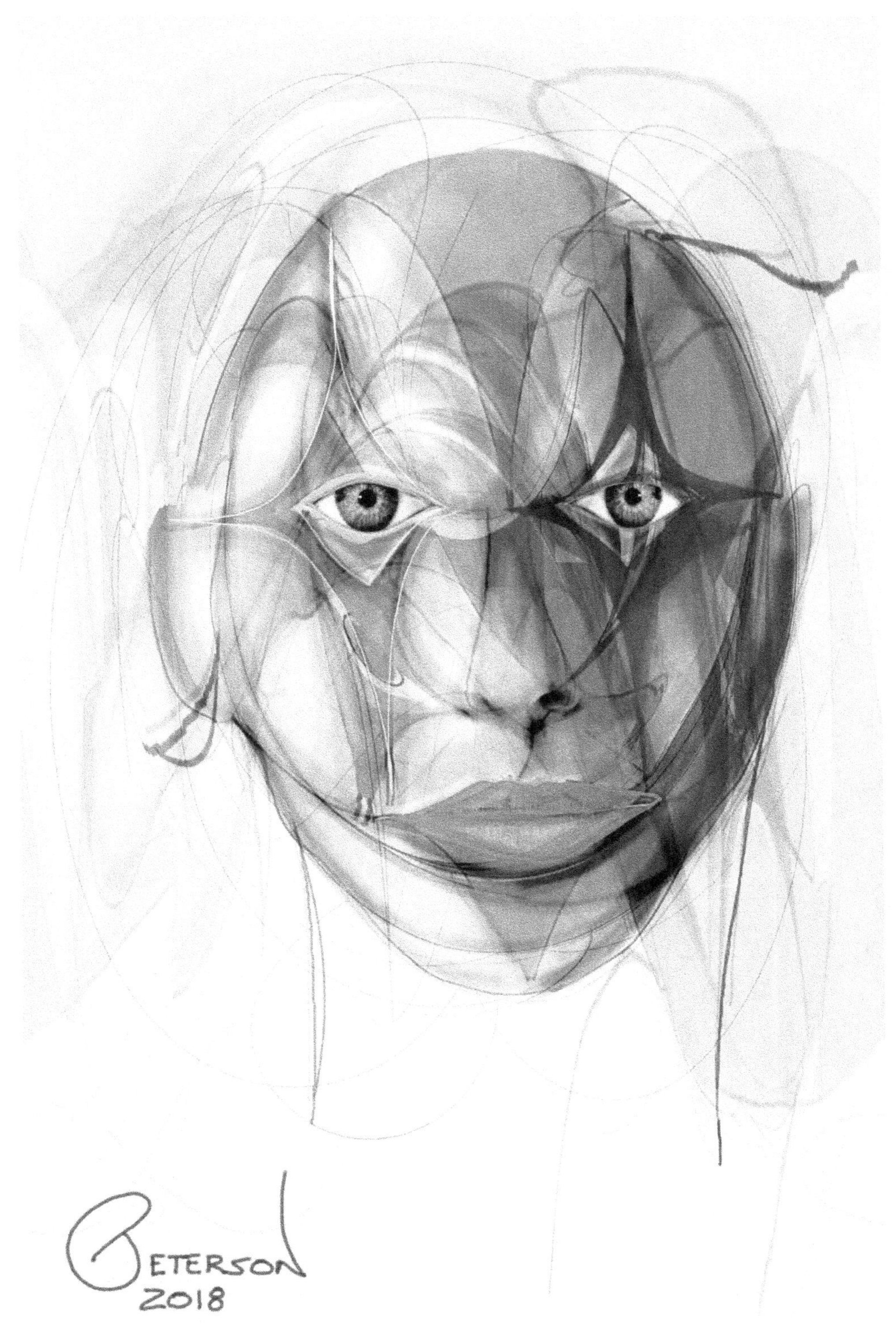

Peterson
2018

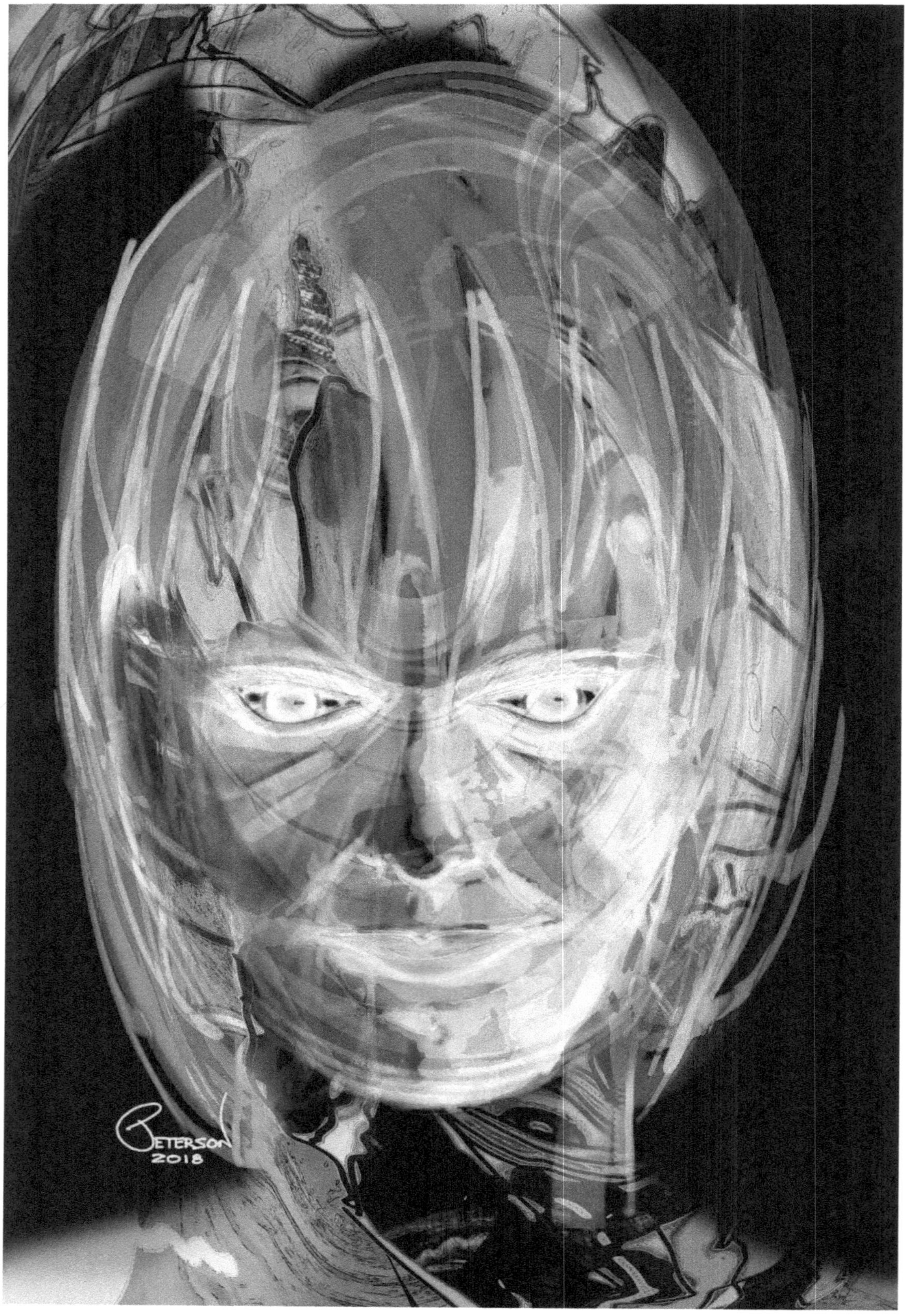

Peterson
2018

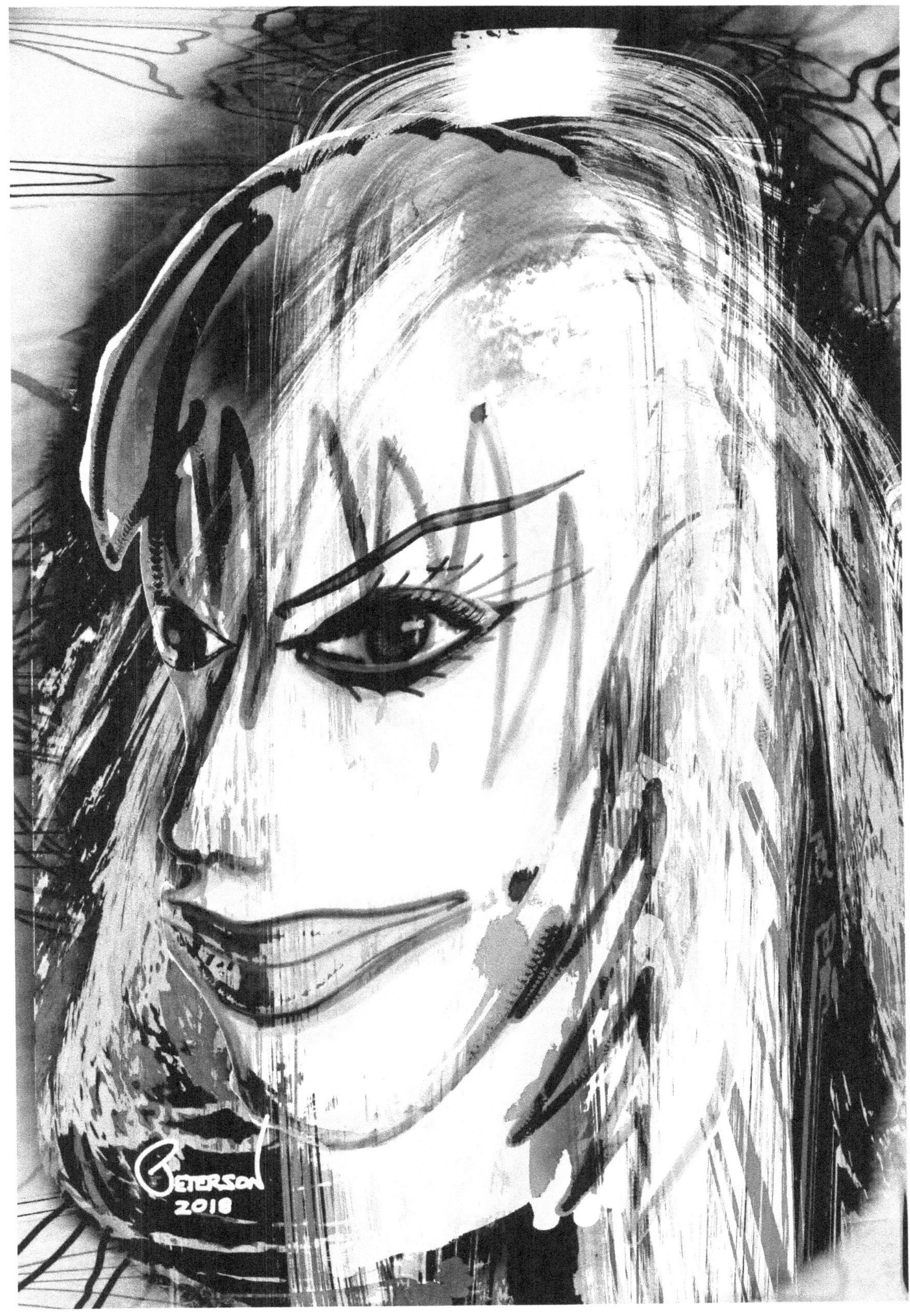
PETERSON
2018

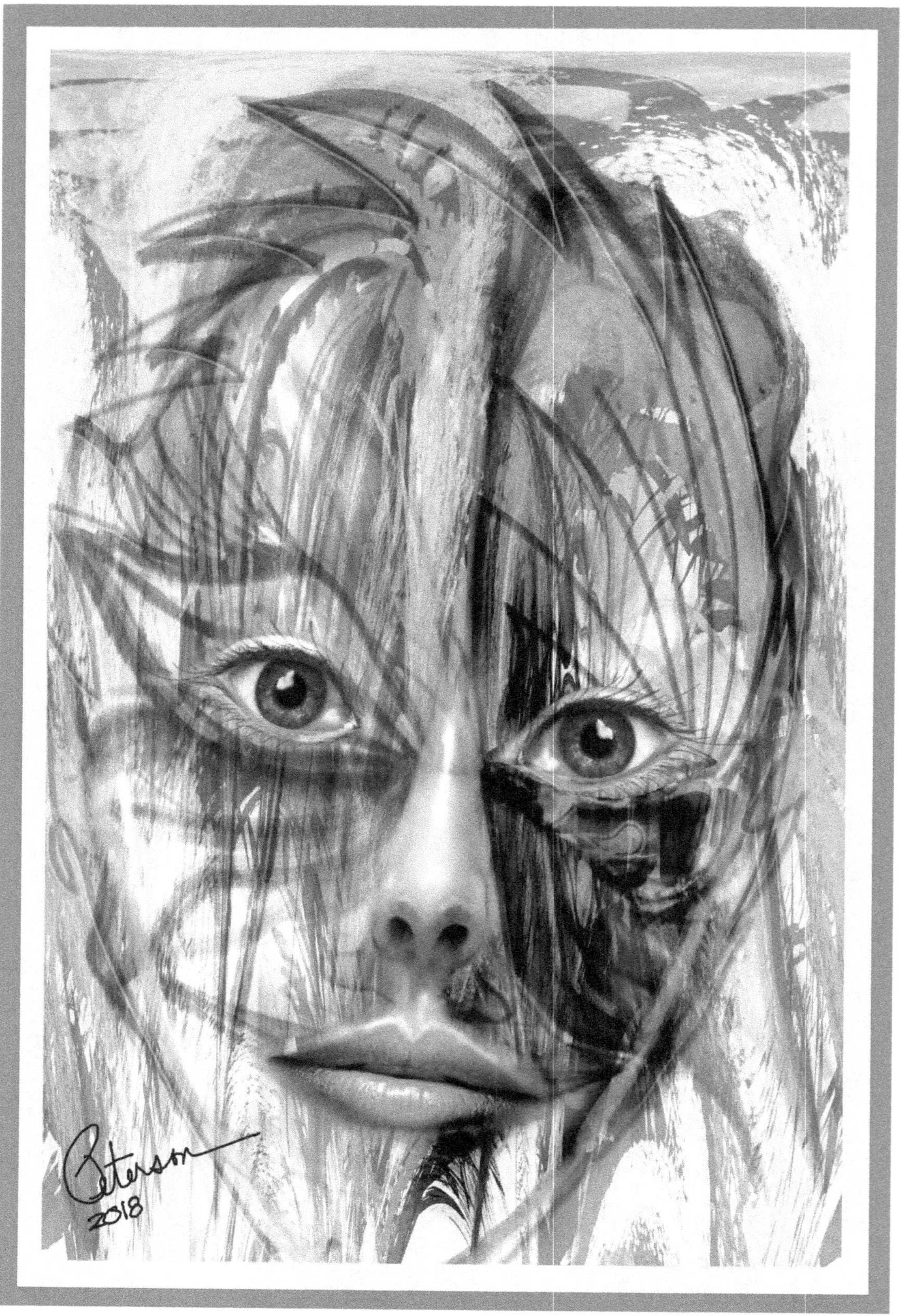
Peterson
2018

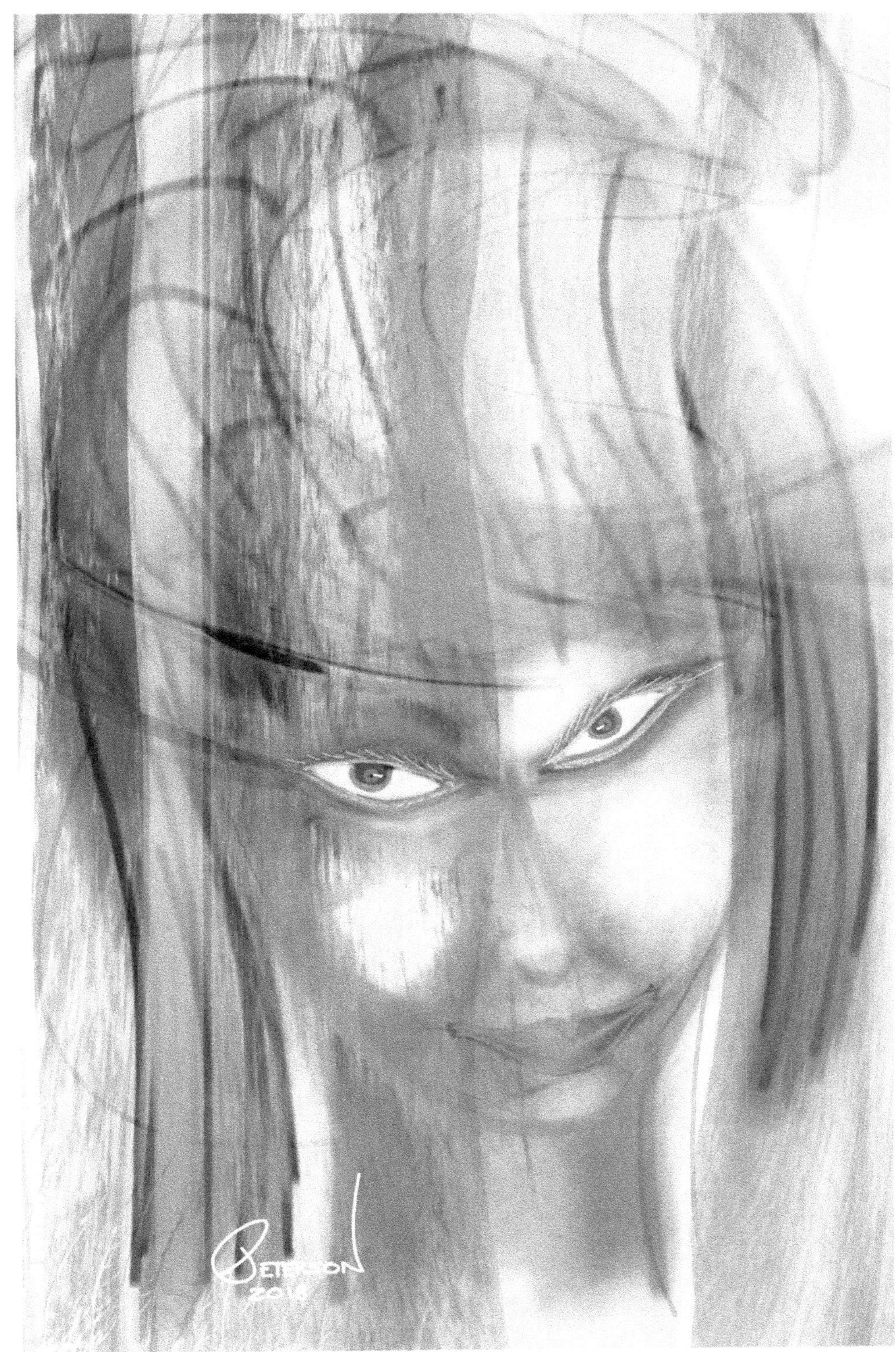

40

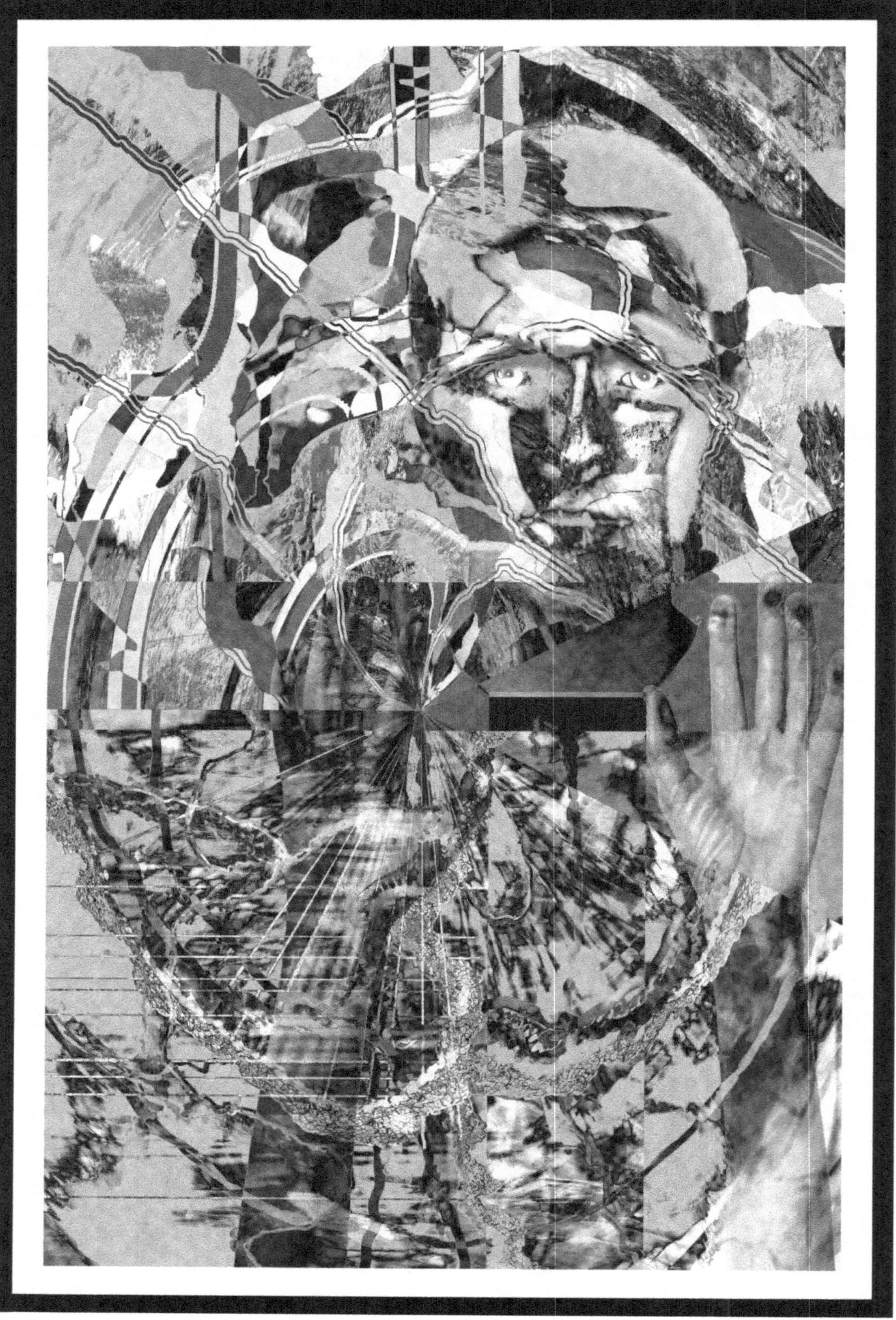

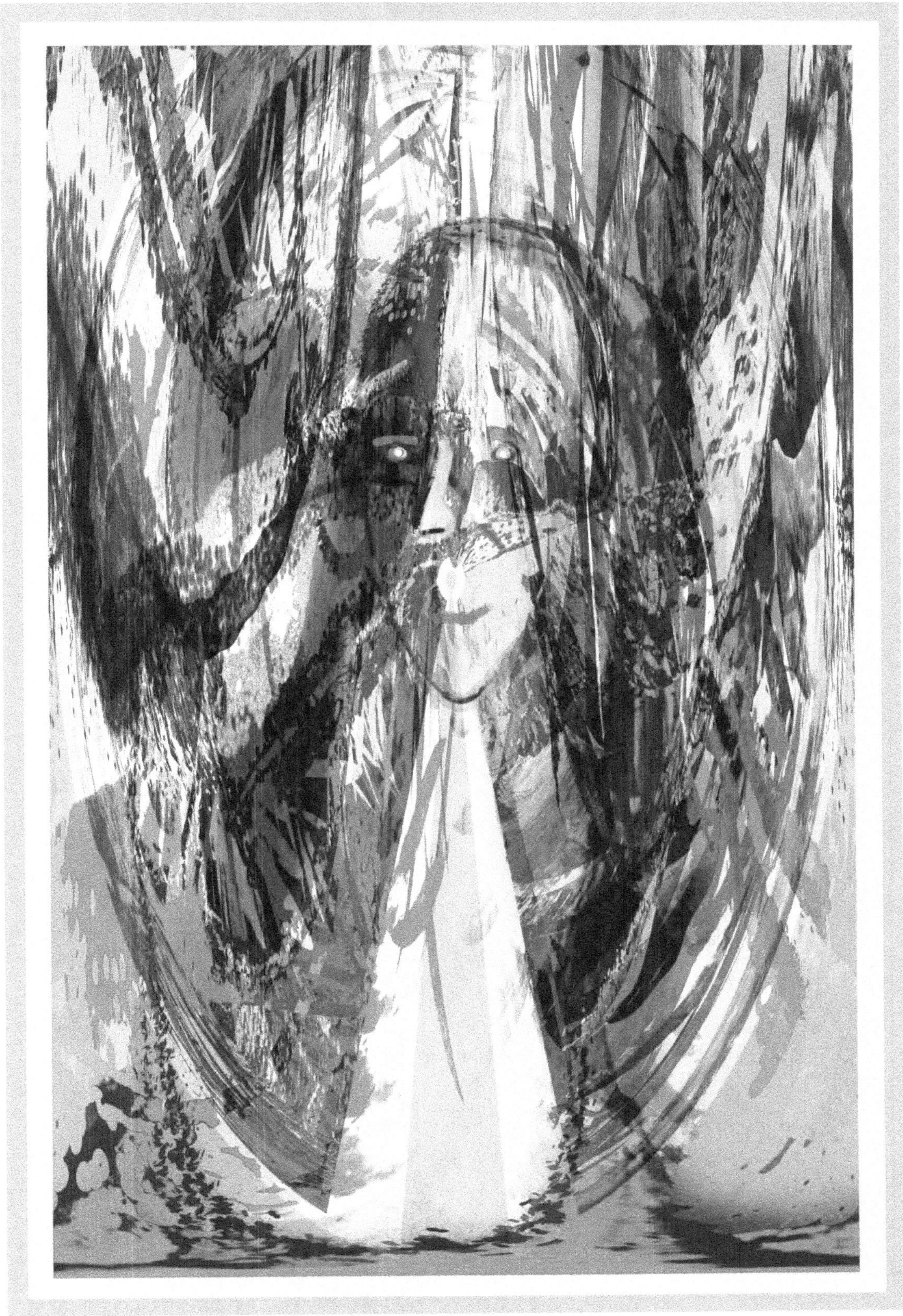

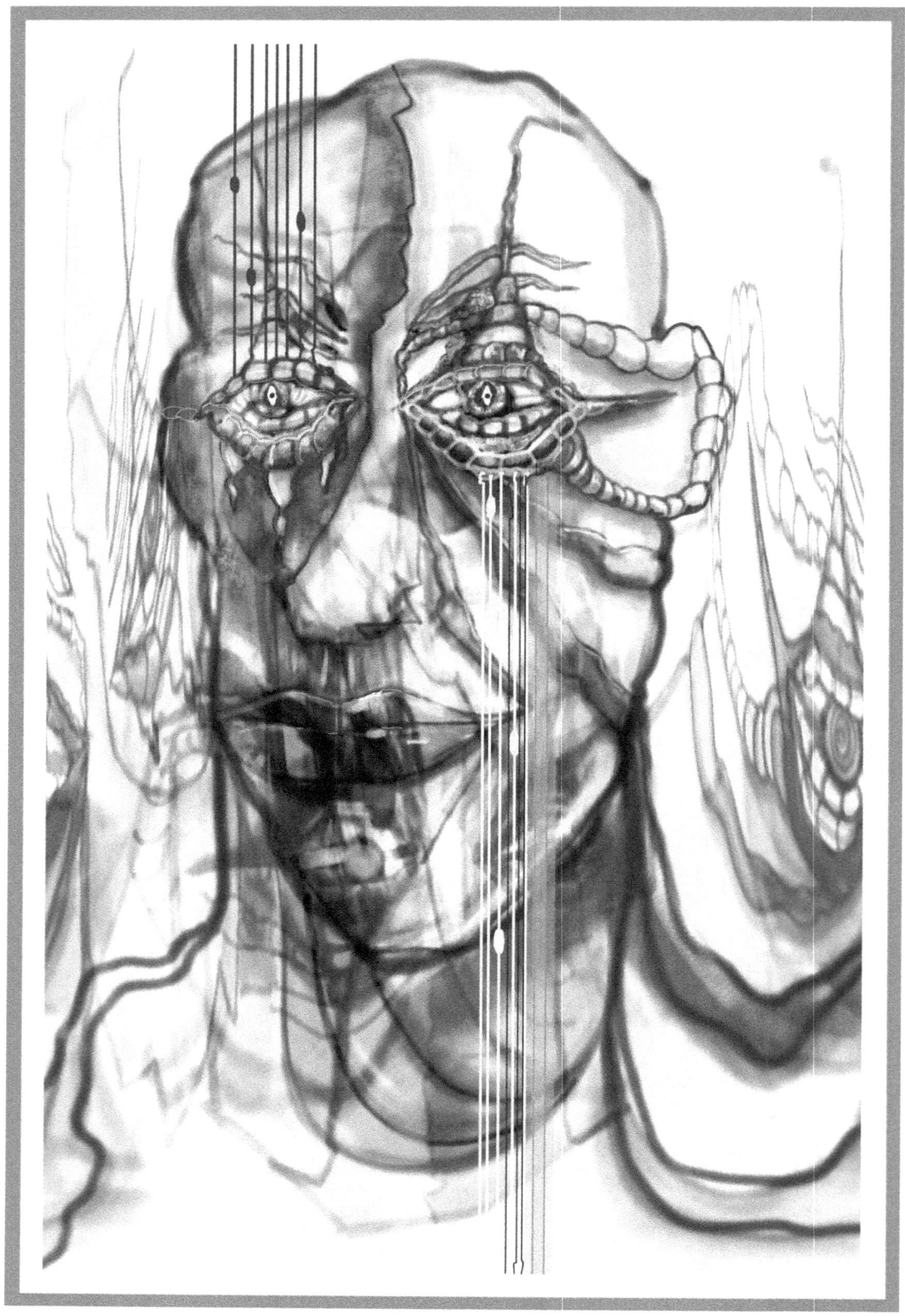

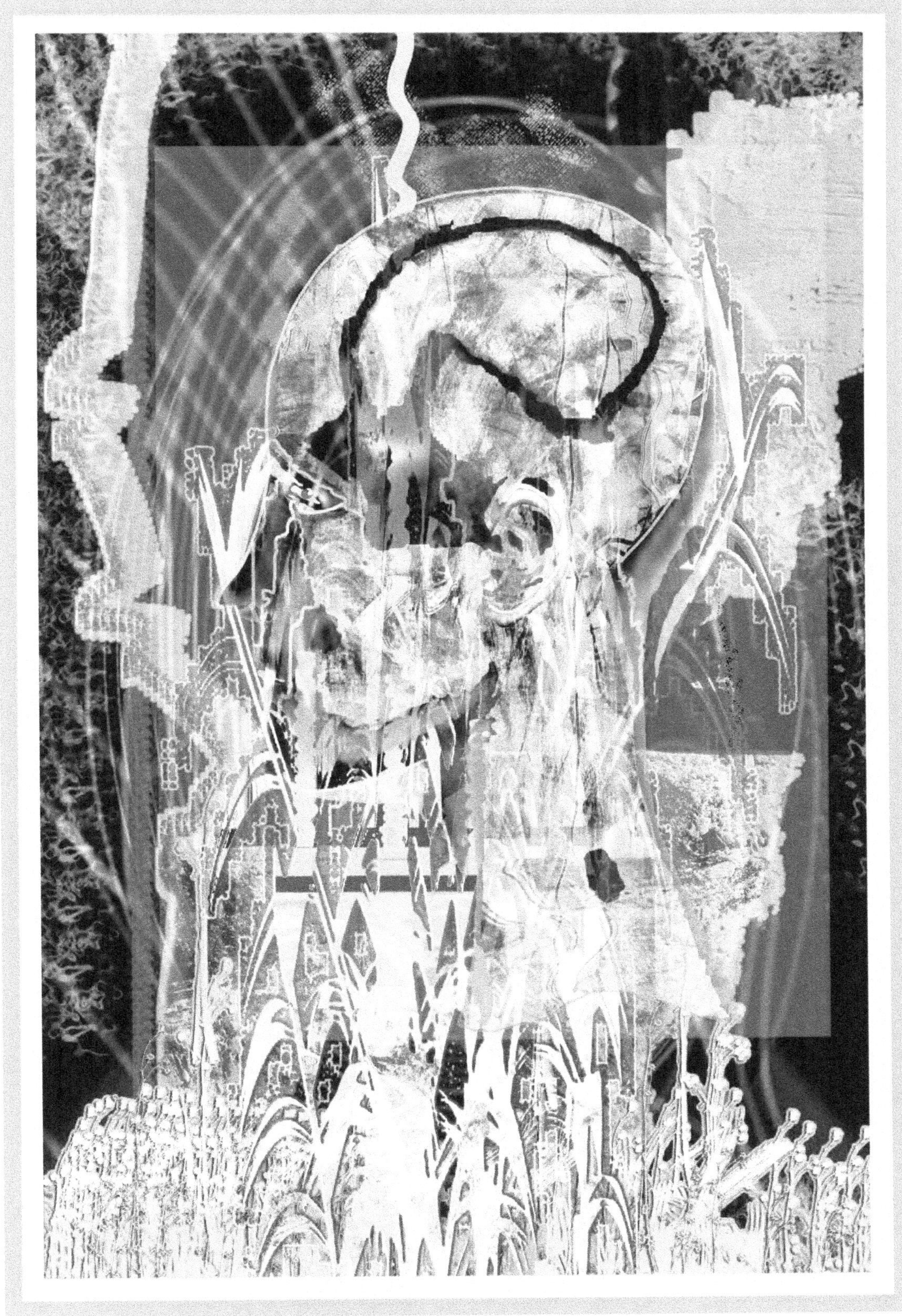

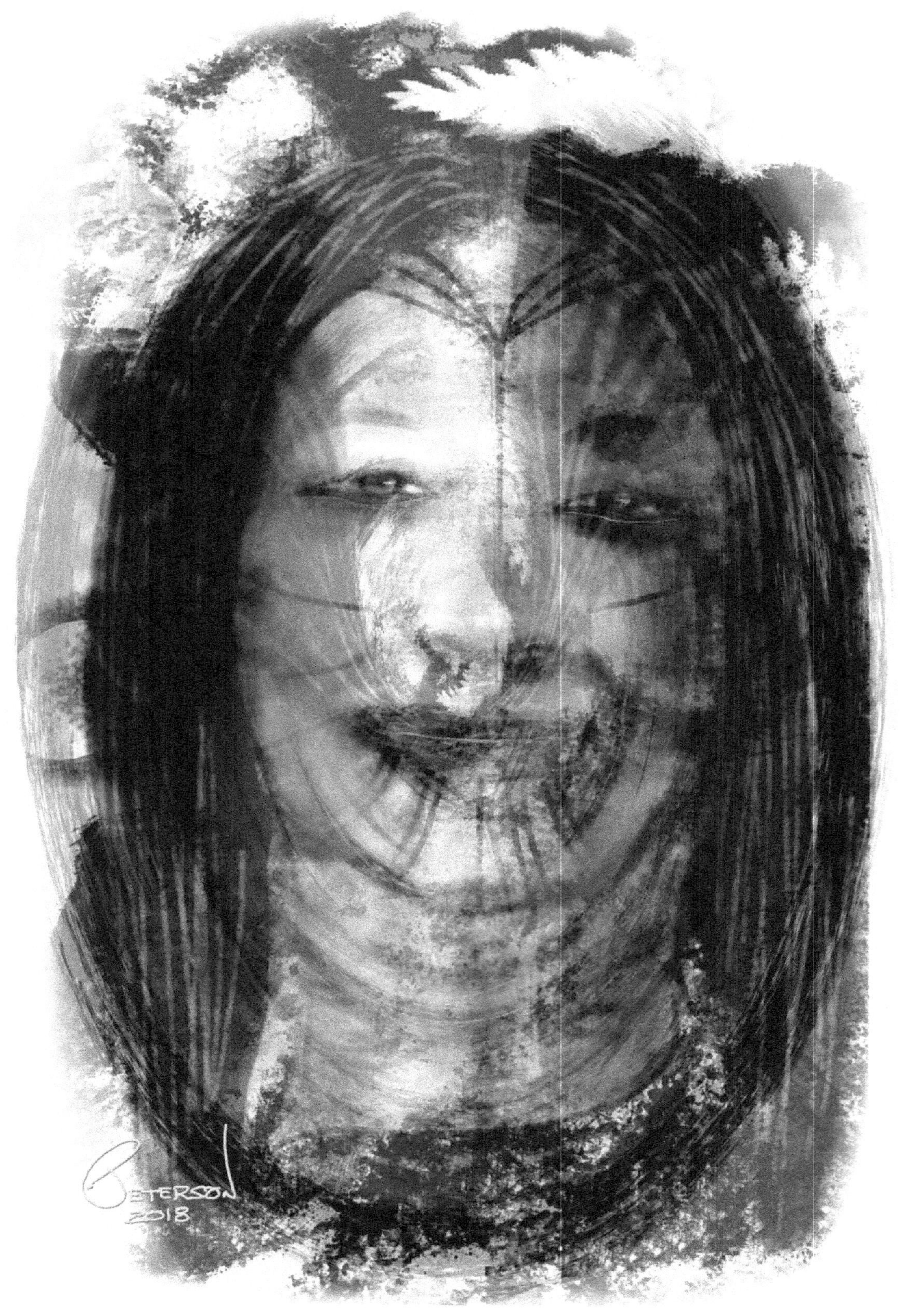

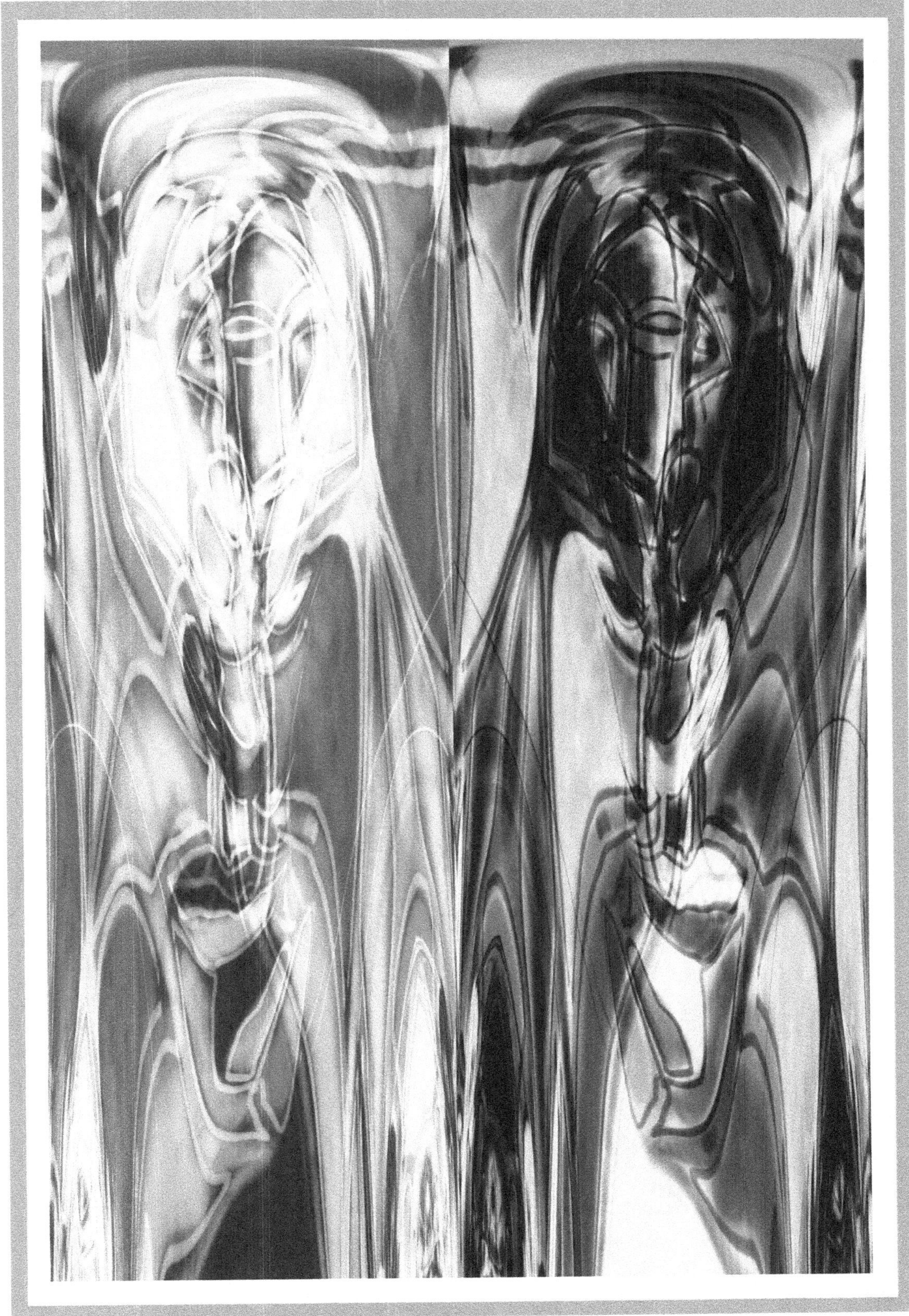

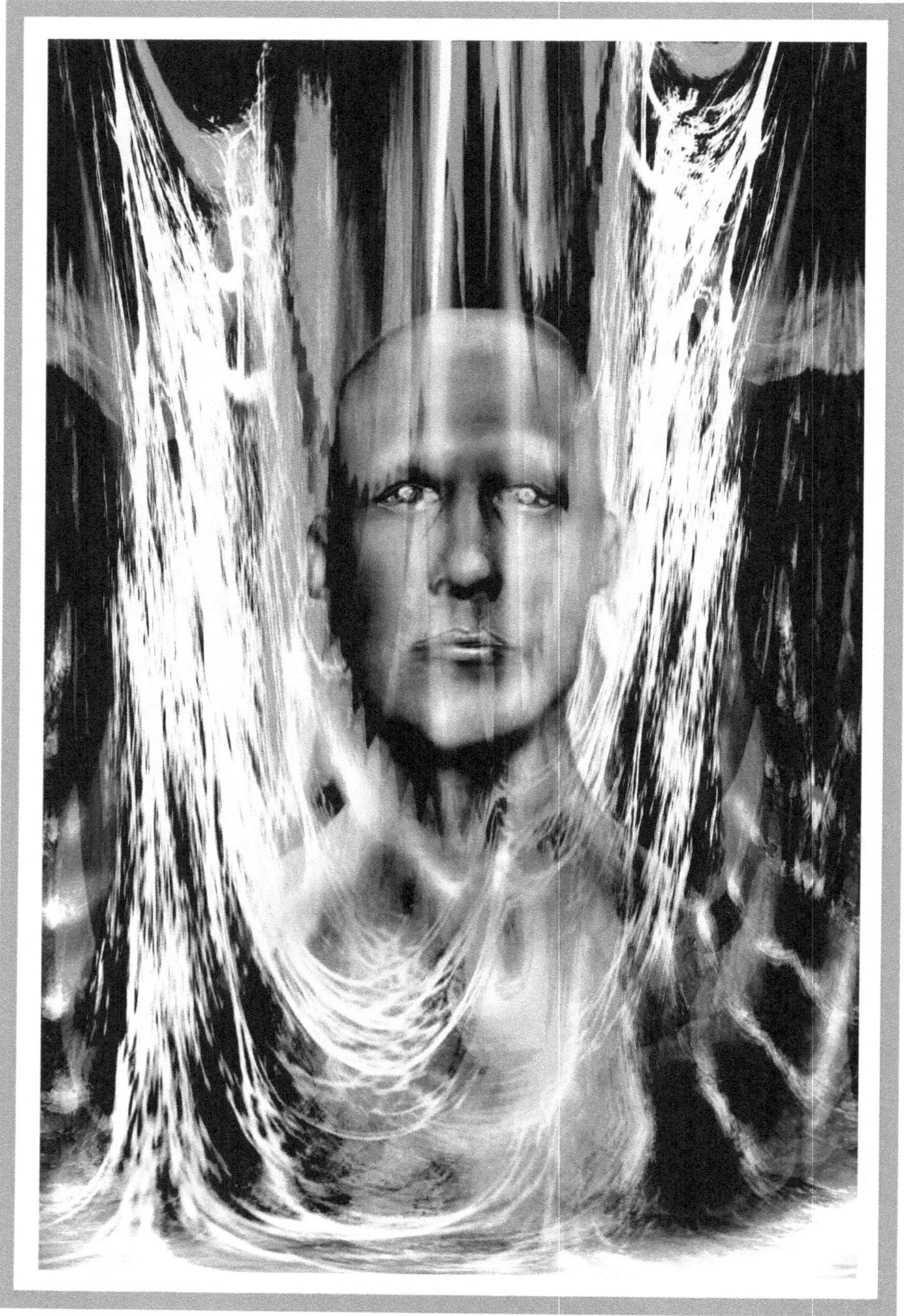

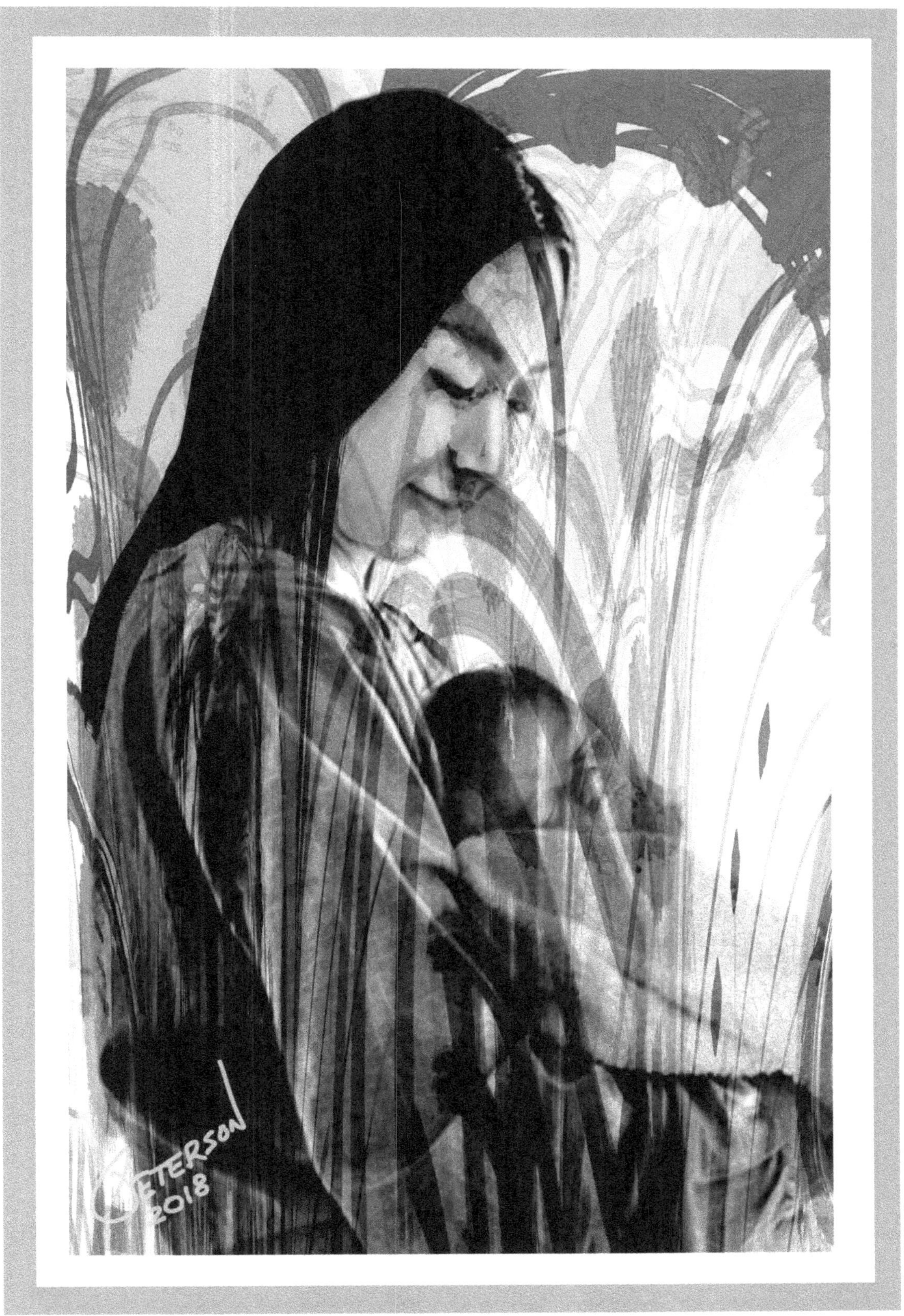

PETERSON
2018

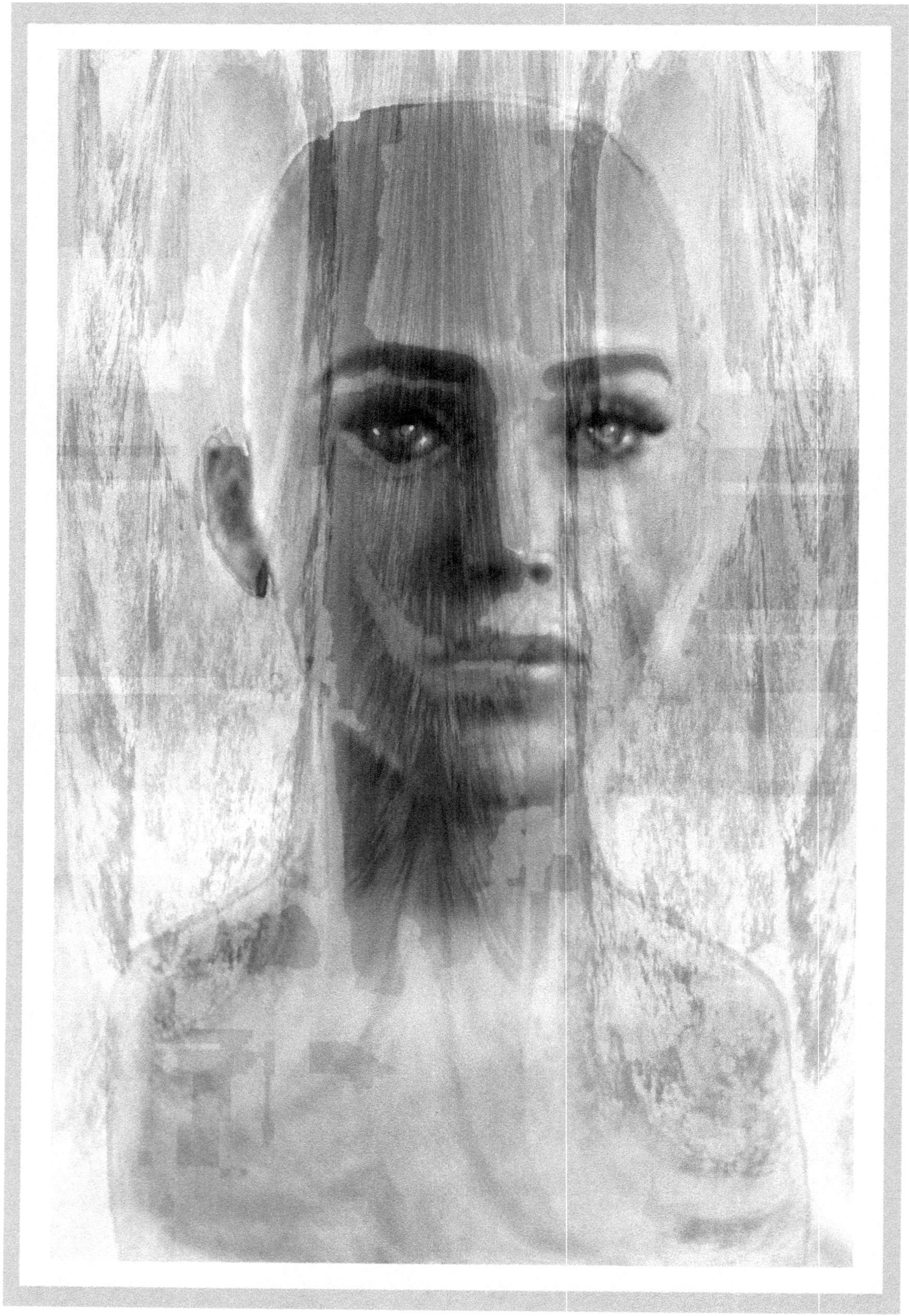

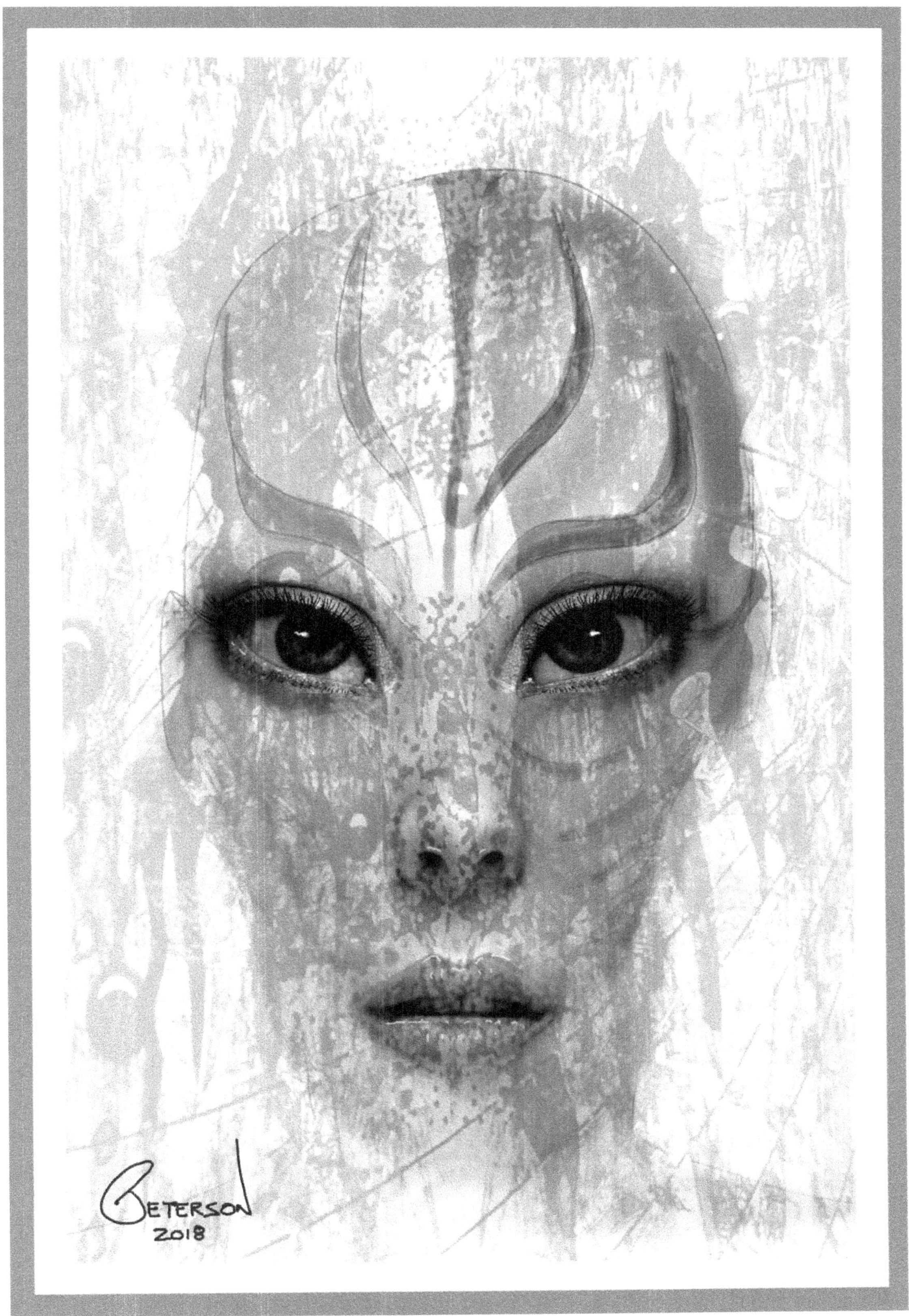

Peterson
2018

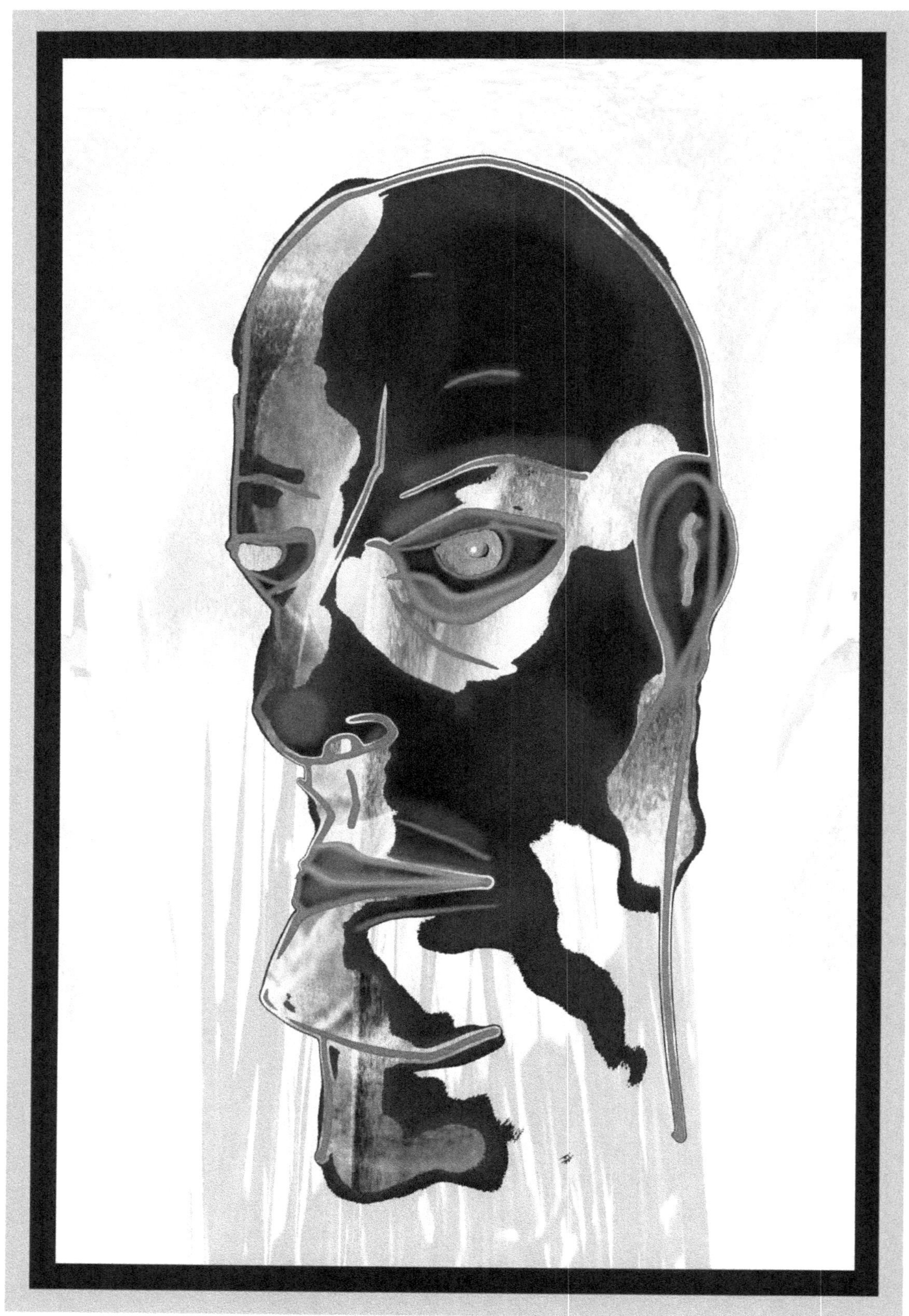

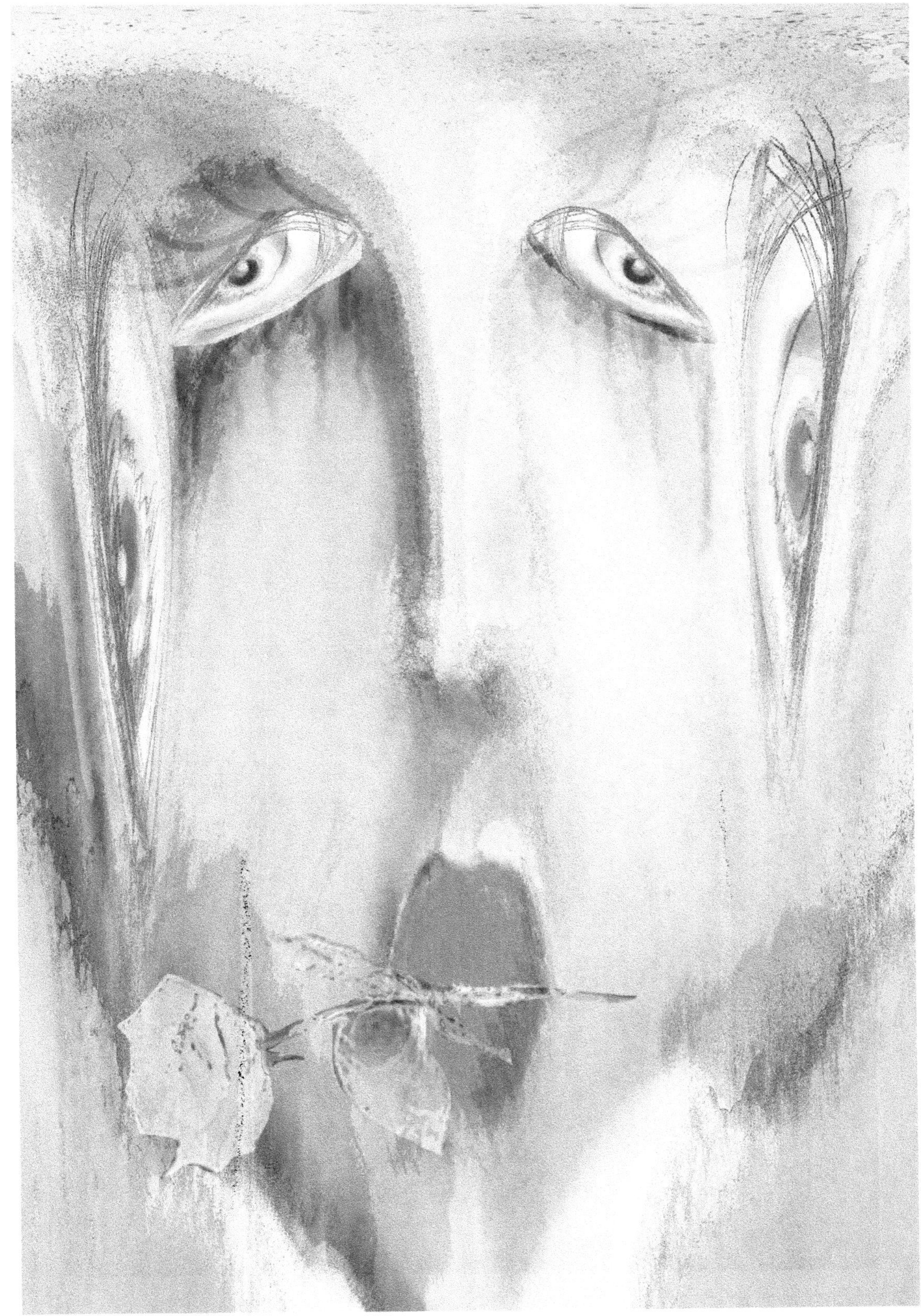

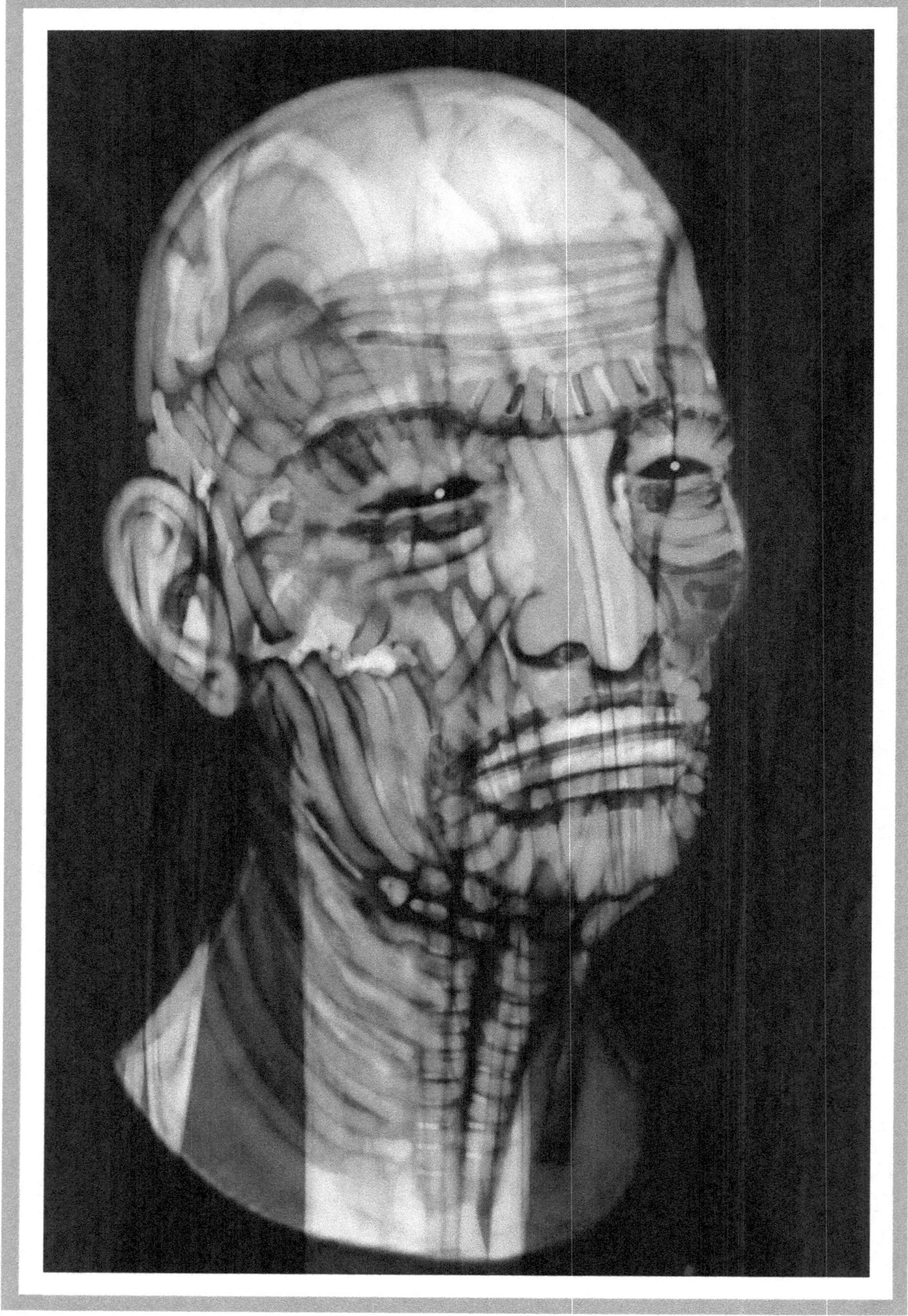

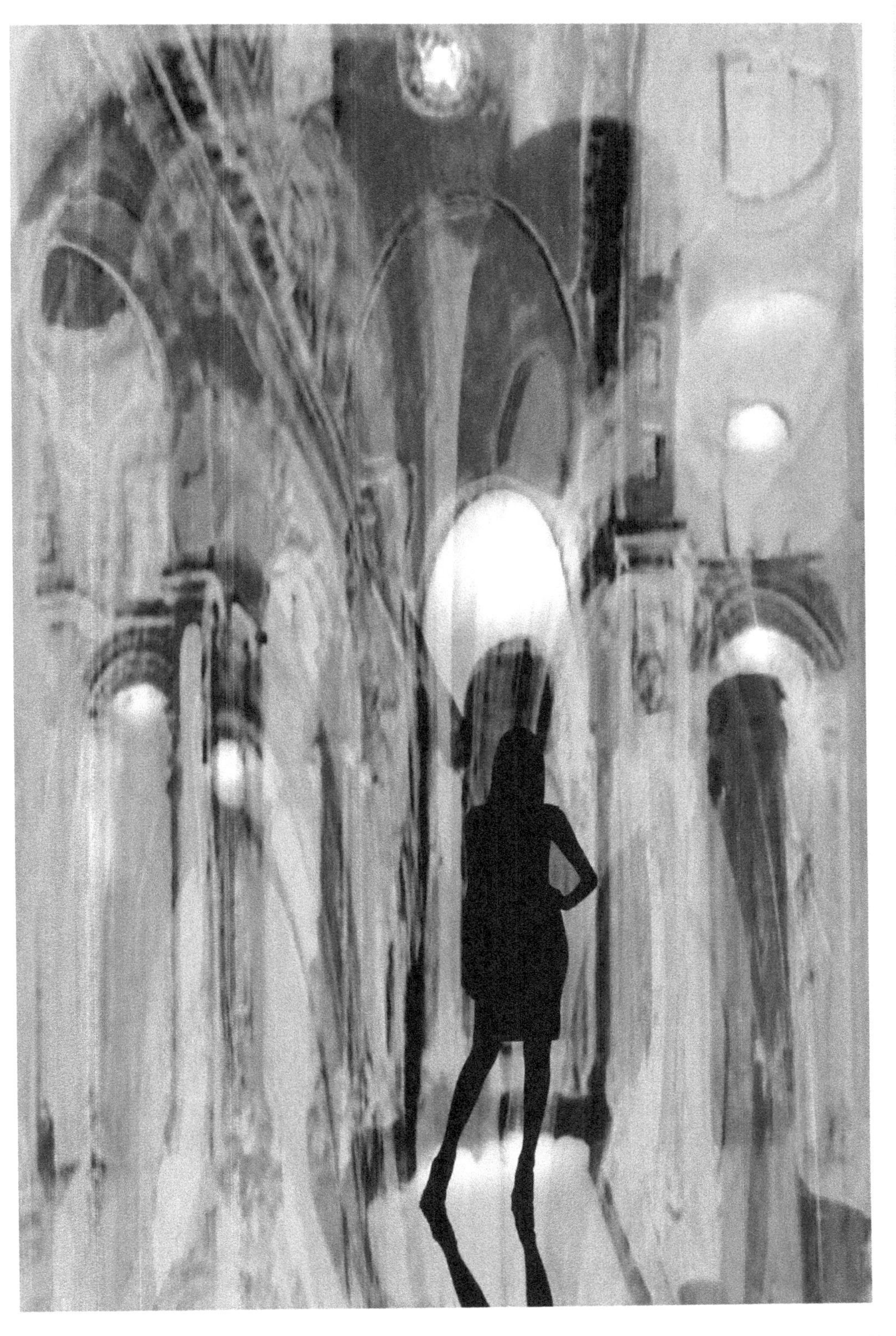

About the Author

Dr. P. is a cognitive psychologist, writer, and artist. His research involves the reticular activating system and cognitive dissonance arousal. His paintings are known for stimulating incongruity to maximize thought provoking insights and new experiences. Welcome to his mind. Please also consider his newest book release, How to Become an Alpha Being ISBN 9780463137499.

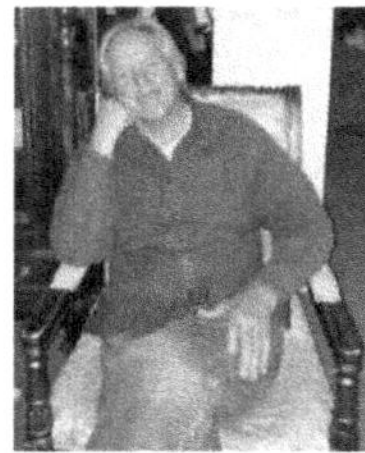

9 781797 751108